HARDEN THE... F#CK UP!

How TO BE RESILIENT,
Stop TAKING THINGS PERSONALLY
AND **Get** WHAT YOU WANT IN LIFE

FELIX ECONOMAKIS

NEW
HOLLAND

A diamond is just a piece of charcoal that handled stress exceptionally well.

Anonymous

CONTENTS

INTRODUCTION

You know what the fellow said – in Italy, for thirty years under the Borgias, they had warfare, terror, murder and bloodshed, but they produced Michelangelo, Leonardo da Vinci and the Renaissance. In Switzerland, they had brotherly love, they had five hundred years of democracy and peace – and what did that produce? The cuckoo clock … and holes in cheese.[1]

– From the film *The Third Man*

Are we getting too soft?

Adversity can be our friend. In the right balance, stress and challenges promote growth and creativity.

In the industrialised world, peace and prosperity are wonderful things. The only downside of that prosperity is that it can make us soft and flabby, both physically and mentally. In this modern age of public transport, cars, technological conveniences like washing machines, and readily available food, we lead a far more sedentary lifestyle than our ancestors, or than people living in the developing world. There is far less need for physical activities, such as walking long distances to get to work, or doing manual labour.

Since muscles grow under a certain amount of stress, our bodies are becoming far flabbier than that of our more physically active ancestors.

---

1. Orson Welles is quoted as saying: 'When the picture came out, the Swiss very nicely pointed out to me that they've never made any cuckoo clocks.' The clocks are actually from in Germany, the 'and holes in cheese' a later addition by an unknown source. Still, the point remains that times of duress produce some great innovations.

Muscles, it turns out, won't hang around if they are not used and applied.

To counter this, many of us have compensated for the lack of adequate physical stress in daily life by going to the gym. We understand that the implicit logic behind maintaining muscles is that we either 'use it or lose it'.

What works for the body also holds true for the mind. But while we readily recognise the need to take our bodies to the gym in order to make up for the lack of physical hardship in modern life, it seems we are having difficulty applying the same thinking to keep our minds, like our muscles, strong.

A few months ago, I watched a programme on TV that filmed four or five unemployed English people being given opportunities to work. The programme came about as a response to a belief held, in some circles, that foreigners were stealing the jobs of native English people. To investigate this claim, the makers of the programme arranged for the unemployed English people to work alongside foreign workers in restaurants, on constructions sites, or fruit-picking.

While not exactly a scientific study, the results of this small 'test group' were very interesting. It soon became apparent that none of the English workers could cope with the stress of the work – whether it was learning the names of new dishes, being organised and punctual, or just the sheer labour of picking fruit. In contrast, the foreign workers were hardworking, committed and far more resilient, both mentally and in terms of physical endurance. So, naturally, UK employers preferred to hire foreign workers. In fact, the owner of the fruit-picking company featured said that he initially tried creating jobs for local people but that it didn't work out, for the same reasons that soon became evident in the programme. Far from stealing the jobs of others, the owner said that if it weren't for his Polish employees, his company wouldn't exist at all, which would certainly be detrimental to the local economy.

Ironically, three of the unemployed English men, who left their assigned jobs because they could not cope with them, were actually regular gym members and very physically fit. But while their bodies were strong, the same could not be said of their minds. They found it easier to fall back on a welfare system designed to protect the disadvantaged and which, in reality, can sometimes end up disempowering the very people it tries to support. This is because (the argument goes) the welfare system has systematically removed the need for striving and perseverance that is born from necessity. The simple truth is that foreign workers, unused to the safety net of a welfare system, were hungrier for employment and more willing to do what it took to get and keep that employment.

Recently, I was talking to one of my friends, a teacher at a large secondary school, who told me, 'My brother, who has his own electrical business, says the resilience of young people coming into his workplace is disgraceful. He says his staff have no initiative or commitment to the job and cannot follow directions from people. It makes me worry about the job we (and I include myself) have done in educating students for an ever-changing world.'

He then went on to give me examples of how he sees young children becoming increasingly 'de-skilled' in the area of resilience.

In England, the National Health Service (NHS) seems to have unwittingly created some of the same problems as the welfare system, in terms of mental health. Many NHS doctors will readily prescribe medication in non-serious cases to dull feelings of stress, uncertainty and normal anxiety, whereas their patients might be better served by developing coping methods to become more resilient at work, or in whatever area they are distressed about.

Just as people who stick to their comfort zones end up becoming more risk-aversive (and so miss out on opportunities to expand and enrich their perspectives and their lives), it seems there is an increasing trend in our society towards becoming 'adversity-aversive' – as if adversity were a nuisance, like a cough, that we need to quickly remove, before somebody complains and threatens to sue us for being exposed to any form of discomfort.

In my consulting work, I see a similar general decline in resilience in many areas – for instance, in the area of relationships. All relationships are challenging, containing as they do two individuals with different expectations, beliefs and values. Some friction between two individuals is natural and to be expected, but it seems people are increasingly throwing in the towel at the smallest obstacles, rather than working through them.

By contrast, in my five years of working in the NHS, I had the chance to talk with many elderly people. One of the things that struck me was how they all seemed to share some common values that suggested greater resolve and resilience in certain areas. In terms of a work ethic, they all appeared to take greater pride in being self-sufficient than the younger patients I saw, and tended to see reliance on state benefits as shameful. If they had occasion to go on benefits in the past, they did so reluctantly and sought to get off them at the earliest opportunity.

Although there are different kinds of resilience in different contexts, in terms of work ethics our elders appear to have more resolve when it comes to attitudes to working, and not being beholden to the state. How is it that the elderly have such different ethics around work? The answer is that they were taught and brought up with different *values* about life.

In very basic terms, values represent the differing levels of pain or pleasure we associate with different things. Our nervous system is designed to pursue pleasure and avoid pain, so the degree of pain or pleasure we have learnt to attach to different things will determine whether we pursue them or withdraw from them. Some people have learnt to associate pleasure with activities that can involve a lot of hard work (e.g. doing work in a garden, organising an untidy room), while others associate pain with those same activities.

One of the key roles of any parent is to educate their children to be able to adapt, function and live in the world around them (i.e. to teach useful values that will help them to survive better in the environment). Children start off being completely dependent on their parents, but this situation cannot last. Parents will not be around forever to look after their children, so in due course children need to learn to stand on their own two feet. Not teaching a child how to manage on her own is to do her a great disservice and skips a vital part of her education. If parents fail to educate their children in these life lessons, they are sending them out into the world ill-prepared and ill-equipped to deal with the harsh realities of life. As these children grow into young adults, they will lack the required tools to deal with the obstacles they face.

It appears that the older generations learned such values and life lessons relatively better from their parents. Ask an older person about the 'realities of life', and they will tend to reply with certain stock answers that illustrate these values, such as: "The world doesn't owe you a living" (you have to be responsible for finding out what you want, and then go and do it); "There are no free lunches" (everyone has a contribution to make); "If you want something, save and work hard"; and "You get back what you put in." Notice the lack of complaining or blaming in such phrases, and the emphasis on personal responsibility. Of course, not every older person is more resilient than every young person. There are big individual differences. I am referring to a general trend around which there seems to be a common consensus.

If older people hold all these useful values, then why is it that these life lessons were not passed down to more recent generations? Somewhere along the line, there seems to have been a break in the chain of communication.

There are many different reasons for this – some in our control, and some not. Some of the older generation did successfully manage to instill useful values in their children, to help them grow up into resilient young individuals. In fact, in my consulting room, I've seen the differences firsthand between patients who are facing a whole litany of physical, financial or circumstantial problems, but who deal with them without complaint and have come to me for assistance on one or two smaller things, while others are overwhelmed and unable to function when faced with far lesser challenges.

Then there are other parents who tried, but whose children were either unwilling or unable to learn these lessons, or for whom the values were diluted by counter-conditioning from some other external source (friends or peer groups with different values, teachers, family members, doting grandparents). Outside influences are not always in our control. We just have to do our best to make a very strong and compelling case for our values in relation to others.

Some parents, however, took (or are taking) a different path, indulging and spoiling their children without any sense of balance or consideration of the long-term effects. At the time of writing, there has been a recent surge of concern about this in the media: for example, that some parents were driving their children to school, when school was only a few hundred yards away. In my travels and own experiences, I have seen children of different cultures not only put up with more hardship and deprivation, but also seem happier than a lot of spoilt or over-indulged children of richer nations. Over-indulged children seem not only harder to please, but are also being trained to be over-demanding.

Why would parents set up their beloved children for needless frustration and disappointment later in their lives?

The reason is because they are reacting emotionally, rather than rationally and strategically. When emotions are dominant, we are more likely to make rash and short-sighted decisions and miss the bigger picture.

Some parents who came from deprived backgrounds spoil their children because they want to give them everything they lacked in their own childhoods. My own grandparents did precisely that to my mother and her brother, my uncle. My grandparents came from a poor mountain village in Greece. They lived through two world wars and a terrible civil war, had to make do with very little, and had to grow up quickly, putting their childhoods on hold to pitch in and help run the household.

As an adult, my grandfather worked hard and ended up owning quite a successful store. When my mother was born, he and his wife could not resist giving her everything. While my mother longed for a measure of independence, and wanted to work as an air hostess, my grandfather was determined that my mother 'would never have to work' and endure the long hours he had experienced. He wanted to give her the childhood he had fantasised about during his years of hardship growing up, in which someone would come and 'rescue' him from all the uncertainty and deprivation. My grandfather was acting out the role of rescuer for my mother, aiming to heal his past vicariously through her.

Consequently, my mother was trained for a world that was easy, affluent and problem-free – in other words, not the real world! As you might guess, there was a huge mismatch between the demands and needs of the real world and the tools my mother was given to face them. She was completely under-prepared, and clueless about how to cope when problems inevitably started to happen in life. She was brought up to think that if problems came up, people around her would fall over themselves to save her. But my grandfather, who had successfully trained her to be dependent on him, could not keep his commitment to her as he grew older, suffered ill health and lost his business. To add insult to injury, my mother was wholly reliant on others to look after her, but hated herself for being this way, and resented her parents. She finally suffered a nervous breakdown from which she never recovered.

As for my uncle, when his own business (which was badly managed) started to fail and his marriage ended acrimoniously, he took his own life, leaving behind a young daughter of three. He didn't have the resilience to see through his difficulties and responsibilities. It was a lose-lose situation for everyone, with parents having unwittingly harmed the very children they loved and wanted to protect, and then suffering in turn from the distress their children were going through.

Now, it's important to be clear that my grandfather and grandmother were good people who loved their children and wanted the best for them. They just didn't know how to teach them to survive and flourish in the world. We all want to protect our children, but we must not let our strong emotional instincts dominate our decisions, because they could have disastrous consequences further down the line.

Let's consider for a moment, by way of analogy, the human immune system. A while back there was a big health drive in the UK to prevent children from being exposed to germs. That kind of makes sense, right? If germs are bad, then the obvious solution is to protect our children from exposure to them (witness the advertisements for cleaning products that promise to kill 99% of bacteria, with cooing babies crawling on pristine floors). So parents would scrub and clean tables and carpets, and if a sweet dropped on the floor, the parent would stop the child from eating it and instead dump it in the bin.

The result? Rather than a generation of robust young adults, the country saw an explosion of asthma, respiratory and allergy problems. Parents were doing too *good* a job in keeping the children away from germs, so that the children's own immunological defence systems were not sufficiently challenged. Consequently, when the children grew older (and the parents were not constantly around to keep the germs at bay), they did not have the antibodies or the experience to fight germs on their own.

The immune system in a growing child acts like a muscle; it grows more under a certain amount of optimal duress. Most of the time, if a child has an infection or virus early in life (e.g. chicken pox), they experience a minor illness and obtain a lifelong immunity to these diseases, which would otherwise cause much more serious problems later in life. Parents have started to realise that they need to step back and allow their children's immune systems to face more adversity in order to develop resilient defences for later life. The same principle applies to the development of emotional and psychological resilience.

Aside from parents, two other major sources of unhelpful values training are schools and the media.

In primary and junior schools, most teachers promote values emphasising inclusion and participation, so that no one feels left out, hurt or rejected. In the UK, many competitive events at school have been stopped because of the concern for the feelings of children who would not be successful in them. Instead, an all-inclusive 'everyone gets a reward for participation ' approach has been cultivated. While this is nice for the playground, it's not the best training for the grown-up world, because when those same children become young adults, they will face a working and life environment with very different rules in place.

In the media, young people are exposed to very dubious role models – for instance, many untalented people who become celebrities purely by virtue of their attention-seeking behaviour or appearing on a reality TV show. One of the most depressing surveys of recent times showed that a majority of young girls' main ambition in life was to 'marry/go out with a footballer'.[2]

These 'celebrities' give children the misleading impression that they can have it all for nothing, because they have witnessed other people being handed fame and fortune on a plate, without the usual striving and perseverance. In turn, an increasing number of young people, also lacking the required talent, appear to have staked their future happiness on making it big as a singer on *X-Factor* or a contestant on *Big Brother*,

---

2. Frith, M 2006, 'Women in twenties spend £1,000 a month on the WAG lifestyle', *The Independent*, 18 July, viewed 13 February 2013, <www.independent.co.uk/news/uk/this-britain/women-in-twenties-spend-1631000-a-month-on-the-wag-lifestyle-408395.html>

and don't seem to have considered a Plan B for when that doesn't work out.

Whenever I watch these reality shows, it's almost invariably obvious to me that their unrealistic expectations are not the fault of these undistinguished children, but the people around them, who have been building them up to believe they will become a star, and instantly rich and famous, regardless of merit. When the judges give these bad performers a long overdue reality check, the contestants find it difficult to take the criticism, because they are not prepared for it. They resort to pathetic pleas to have another attempt at their dream, or become aggressive and want to shoot the messenger (all of which, of course, provides the dramatic 'entertainment' on which such shows depend).

To make matters worse, this seemingly general decline in resilience among the younger generations is also happening at a time when we need to be more resilient than ever, to deal with the difficult modern challenges facing us today: economic uncertainty; more job competition with less job security; a need for increasing diplomacy as we live shoulder to shoulder among more diverse cultures and customs. We need to harden up and we need to do it now.

Given the mismatch between the demands and needs of the real world, and the tools recent generations have been equipped with to face them, this book was written with the aim of addressing the gap.

What is resilience?

Simply put, resilience is the ability to cope with stress and adversity.

Think of your life as a process that churns out an endless variety of problems for you to face. Some are large, some are small, but all make demands on your attention, your energy levels, your mood and your overall wellbeing. In fact, your satisfaction in life largely depends on how you interpret or respond to its demands. I have seen both miserable multi-millionaires, and happy people of very modest means.

Resilience is a quality that will reduce the impact of the challenges you face in your life. The more resilient you are, the quicker you will bounce back from adversity, the better you will cope with life's problems, and the more energy you will have at the end of the day.

People who lack sufficient resilience look like they are in a constant state of tension, worry and gloom. I call this the 'siege mentality'; they feel constantly besieged and overwhelmed by enemies on all sides. When we feel besieged or under attack, we tend to withdraw to disconnect from the source of the pain. We retreat to our comfort zones. We also become so occupied with 'survival mode' that we forget to pay attention to the bigger picture and the other blessings we have in our life. We may have good health, beautiful houses, gardens, parks or other lovely things in our lives, but we are not connected to them. Instead it's as if we live in a parallel universe full of fear and ugly surroundings, with no redeeming value. In this weakened, 'un-resilient' state we lose our perspective, humour and connection with the world around us.

Resilient people, on the other hand, tend to be more balanced, more at peace, and enjoy their lives more. They are cooler and more philosophical under pressure. They look younger, because stress hasn't taken the same physical toll on their bodies. They tend to smile and joke a lot more. A person with good resilience might get stressed and become temporarily unbalanced by an adverse event, but quickly regains their composure.

Even better, over time, resilience serves to 'harden up' an individual. By 'harden', I don't mean it makes them bitter and twisted; it 'steels' them for challenges and strengthens their resistance to stress and adversity. In future, they won't even lose their cool in the first place, and stress is like water off a duck's back. It's like having a version of stress inoculation.

In short, think of the default state of un-resilient people as anxiety, frustration, feeling overwhelmed and not coping. Occasionally they manage something better than expected, but they tend to revert to a negative attitude of 'I can't deal with this stress'. In contrast, the default state of resilient people is coping. A sudden unexpected source of stress may derail them, but they revert to the positive attitude of: 'I CAN handle this. Let's take it one step at a time'. They believe and act as if they can systematically dismantle any problem. This also makes them more optimistic.

There are additional physical benefits to developing mental resilience. A fortified mind seems to fortify the body. During times of stress, the sympathetic nervous system (SNS) begins to take over, and the stress response is nothing more than a switch from building to breaking things down. From the body's point of view, building for the future is no longer a priority in the face of an immediate threat to survival – why worry about vulnerability to infection later, it thinks, if your life hangs in the balance in the present moment? Resources are therefore channelled away from maintaining the immune system, leaving us more vulnerable to infection.

With less energy spent on worrying, procrastinating and guilt, the body's immune system is able to function without interference, meaning resilient and optimistic people get ill less frequently and bounce back quicker when they do.

Best of all, resilience is a learnable skill.

Using this book

This book will walk you through six key ways to increase your resilience. I have come to understand these skills based on personal experience and from observing the resilience of others I admire.

I have also included teaching tales and metaphors I have picked up along the way. I like to collect the snippets of wisdom I come across, in the same way some people like collecting postcards. These little gems of wisdom have helped me through my darkest times, saving me a lot of needless heartache, or at the very least, a lot of wasted energy and time. I would like to share them with you and hope they will offer you the same benefits that they have done for me.

Bearing in mind that, for the vast majority of our existence, the wisdom of our elders was passed down to us in a 'right-brained' way via tales and stories around the campfires, I'm a great fan of using analogies and metaphors to illustrate my points, so you will be seeing a lot of that.

It is also important to note that while the six skills are linked to each other in various different ways, they are all necessary if you want to develop good general resilience, and are best learnt in the order and sequence presented, rather than in isolation. To bring this point home, here's a quick analogy (I told you there'd be a few of these!).

Suppose an individual came to me for advice – let's call him Mike. Mike has just been promoted in his company and his new job role requires a lot of presentations, but Mike has a block with public speaking. The first thing I would check is whether Mike is *capable* of doing a presentation, i.e. his ability to organise and prepare notes,, whether he knows how to raise and project his voice, etc. If he doesn't, then he won't be able to achieve his goal. I would then coach him in how to achieve these skills.

Even if Mike learnt how to make good notes and project a good voice, however, he would still fail in presentations if he didn't *believe* in himself as a worthwhile speaker. If Mike feels that his content is inadequate or that people won't like it, he will still have a block about speaking. If this were the case, I would do some work with Mike to change his beliefs in this area.

After our training, Mike would possess both the *capability* (how to prepare good notes, how to use his voice to convey his message) and the *self-belief* (he now actually believes that his content is good enough) he needs, and could well agree that he was now a good speaker … but he may *still* have a block if he personally does not value public speaking as one of his skills. He may, for instance, divert all his attention to administration or other tasks and fail to apply his skills to presentations. And in this case, if Mike wanted to keep his job, he would agree to work with me so I could help him change his values around speaking.

The point of this analogy is to show that Mike needs to develop a combination of skill sets, with each one learned opening the way to the next level of progress, until he finally achieves the outcome he wants. I think of the six core skills described in this book in much the same way.

Each chapter includes a suggested exercise or technique to develop the quality of resilience being discussed, and will end with a brief recap of the points made. The book itself concludes with a chapter of suggestions for how to apply these key points in the areas of relationships, career, parenting, sports and schooling.

Remember: with a little resilience you can weather and solve some problems; with a lot of resilience, you can endure and solve *all* your problems.

So now you are ready to harden up – let's begin!

CHAPTER 1: ATTITUDE

It is our attitude at the beginning of a difficult task, which, more than anything else, will affect its successful outcome.

– William James

Good and bad attitudes

Imagine you want to go out with an attractive young man or woman, or that you are attending a job interview for a job you really want. If you approach either of these situations with a 'bad' attitude (e.g. arrogant, unengaged, rude), you know you will have severely sabotaged your chances of success. So what do you do? Just say you ask your best friend for advice on adopting the right attitude. You might say, 'Mary, what's the best way to ask a girl out?' or 'Mike, if you were interviewing me, what would you be looking for in an applicant?'

If so, well done. You have done a bit of research to find out the most successful attitude to adopt to get something you really desire.

Guess what? We are going to start by doing the same thing here. Instead of the right attitude to get the attractive girl/boy or the great job, we want to find the right attitude for success in life. We also need to know how to keep the girl/boy and the great job, not just get them and rest on our laurels.

So let's agree on some kind of working definition for 'success in life'. What constitutes success in life for you? Let's keep it simple. I expect that, like most people, you:

> want to be happy
> want a good job
> want a nice partner
> want to live in a nice home
> want to be able to afford to go on some nice holidays, pay for your hobbies, etc.

Here I am also supposing that achieving all these things is largely up to you. Even if, as a young adult, you are currently receiving some financial help from your parents, in most cases it may not be enough, and achieving all these desirable things will still mainly rest on your shoulders.

Back to our earlier analogy. If you want to woo the pretty girl, there are certain things you will need to do – make an effort with your appearance, take an interest in her passions, maybe buy her some flowers, etc. If you want the desirable job, you need to look your best, swot up on the company, anticipate and rehearse some questions, and make sure you are punctual.

Basically, there are certain requirements present for getting the things you want. You must figure out what you need to do and then be prepared to do it. For anything you want, there is a price to be paid.

Part of having a 'right' attitude is accepting the price that needs to be paid to get the goods, and working out how to pay that price in the most cost-effective and efficient way possible. A 'right' attitude is pragmatic and solution-focused in its nature.

So, you want the good things in life and you accept that there will be a price. What *is* the price you need to pay and are you prepared to pay it?

The price of the good things

I don't wish to get into a debate here about the many different ways of being happy. For example, if you wished, you could reject modern consumer culture and live in an idyllic little village somewhere, working with your hands. In this case, your needs and cost of living would be very low. But I am assuming that most readers will, by and large, want to live and work in their countries of origin (and there isn't enough room for all of us on those tropical beaches or Tuscan fields anyway). If you want a nice home these days, and everything that goes with that, such as bills, taxes and upkeep, then that costs money, and good money comes from a good job.

Good jobs are desirable. There is competition for them – either from many people wanting the same job or, if self-employed, people competing for the same business. To have a good job you will need to work hard to *get* the job in the first place (training, qualifications, work experience, job interviews), and then work hard to *keep* and *succeed* in the job (pleasing your customers, meeting targets, earning your salary/ revenue increases). Even if the job you want is to be a homemaker, trust me, you will need to work hard in other ways as you project-manage multiple demands.

In short you have asked of Life, 'What do I need to do to get your rewards and be happy?' and Life has replied, 'You will need to work hard.'

Life would also probably add, if it was being honest, 'It's going to be difficult. I am very challenging. I'm going to test you on multiple fronts. I am also going to test different people in different ways. Some people will have it easy financially, but be tested in other ways. Some will be challenged financially, but have it easier in other ways. Some will be tested on every level! Hey, who said I was fair? That's just the way I am. Get used to it. There are reasons why everyone has a different set of challenges before them, but I'm not going to tell you why. Just mind your own business and the plate set before you, and never mind what everyone else is doing. It's your choice to engage with me or drop out.'

The crucial question Life has for you is therefore: 'Are you prepared to pay the price to get the good things you want?'

Take a moment to think about that.

If you said 'yes', then well done, you have the right attitude. That's a good start. If you said 'no', re-read this chapter, get a second or third opinion on my points so far, or perhaps pick this book up at a later time, when Life has given you a bit of a reality check. Because if you think you can cheat the system, think again.

If you are holding out for an inheritance, or you plan to marry a millionaire, or you're going to get rich and famous on a TV talent show, then I hope that works out for you, but I would strongly advise you to have a backup plan. What happens to your wonderful inheritance if your parents make a bad investment, or need expensive long-term medical care, or there is a stock market crash, or a property slump, or a competitor takes away all their business, or your parents have a change of heart and donate it all to charity, or decide to marry someone 30 years younger and give it all to them? All of those things have happened before. As for marrying a millionaire, there is obviously no guarantee of that; likewise if you are staking everything on becoming the latest pop sensation, you had better be truly talented and driven (and lucky: the entertainment and sports worlds are littered with countless 'next big things' who never fulfilled their early promise). And even then, there is still a lot of hard work and resilience needed. Even top performers cancel concerts due to exhaustion and being overworked.

Very, very few people in life get free rides.

So, assuming you have by now (1) *realised* the price for success for the good things in life and (2) *accepted* it and are *prepared* to pay it (thus adopting the right attitude to reach your goal), the rest is in theory very simple. You are at point A and you want to get to point B, because you like point B. What mostly remains, then, is to remove the obstacles in the path to point B. Going back to my earlier public speaking analogy, in the introduction, you may have accepted the price for the kind of success you want, and are prepared to pursue it, but that success may still not happen if you don't know how to do other things, like manage your emotional state or trust yourself to succeed. If you have not sufficiently mastered these things, then these will be pitfalls along the way that may stall your progress, or even discourage you completely from pursuing the success you want. The rest of this book is about preparing you to overcome these pitfalls so that you can pursue your goal without hindrance.

Where does developing resilience come into all this? Well, resilience emerges naturally once you have adopted the right attitude. It's like a huge dormant reservoir of power waiting to mobilised, but only under specific instructions from you. A dramatic universal example of this is, of course, being a parent, especially a mother. If you haven't had a child yet, you may be excused for any ignorance about how much effort it takes to raise one – but I can tell you, anyone who has a child (and has raised this child without an army of helpers and nannies) is demonstrating remarkable resilience. And if you already have a child and have *deliberately* planned for another, then you are going into a stressful situation with your eyes open.

When my wife and I were talking about having a second child, my wife was fully aware of what she would be putting herself through. Firstly there would be the 'cost' of pregnancy: the morning sickness (and my wife tends to have sickness that lasts for months), the discomfort, the inconvenience of restricted movement, and tiredness in day-to-day life. Then there was the birth itself, which would be unavoidably painful. There is a real risk of caesarean, infections, complications, even death. While the last is relatively rare in modern hospitals, other mothers around the world are still bravely prepared to face this torturous experience without the benefit of modern facilities.

After the baby was born, there would be the demands of looking after him or her – the sleep deprivation (which itself has knock-on effects); the tediousness of preparing and washing stuff that the baby needs; the sheer exhaustion and chaos. Later there might be school fees to contend with, which would mean big financial sacrifices. There is the worry of we could afford all the things a young child needs nowadays. I would have to work longer and harder in my business, and have just one week of holiday in summer (as I'm self-employed).

We both knew, in a stone-cold-sober way, the challenges we would be getting into. We knew we would be going through all that work, which we'd already done with our first child, all over again; in fact, as a friend of mine accurately remarked, 'having two children doesn't double the work, it squares it'. And yet we wanted the good stuff that comes with having a child – the love, the connection, finding out about the little being we had created, and the relief of not consigning my first child to be an 'only' with no one to play with. In short, like most parents, we looked at what we wanted, looked at the cost of having what wanted, decided to go forth, and so gave a very clear message to our internal systems: 'Boys and girls, prepare for war again. It's going to be hard, it's going to be chaos, it's going to be stressful… get ready.'

Putting this into action means, for instance, that when the baby has woken you up for the third time in a row that night, you get up and do the job, regardless of how hard it is, because you know you chose this and you agreed to pay the price. There is no complaining, there are no victims here. It's part of the paying the agreed price, but accepting that attitude makes things a lot easier to bear.

If you are a young reader, or just haven't had a baby to relate to my little story, then let me illustrate this point in another way.

Think of something you find boring and tedious to do. If you are at school, think of your most boring lesson or the dullest textbook you have to read. If you are at work, think of some tedious administrative task you loathe. If you manage to face the undesirable task (rather than put it off and avoid it), then you do so by a sheer effort of will. You force yourself to endure, and find the process tedious, boring and painful.

Now think of something you really like to do. Maybe it's reading a Harry Potter book, which could be twice the length of your school textbook. It could be playing a video game for four hours, diligently repeating the same level over and over again until you crack it and reach the next level (where the whole process starts over again). It could be playing some kind of sports. My nephews play football every Sunday morning – that means they have to get dressed, leave a warm house for a cold, usually rainy morning (hey, this is England after all), exert themselves and run around for over an hour, all while being prepared to be tripped over, bruised and scraped, yet they don't complain. The motivation to endure all comes naturally from knowing that they want to play football, that football makes them happy, and that they are happy to pay the price for playing it.

Or think of the queues of cheerful people who camp out on the pavement in the early hours of the morning to queue for the latest Apple iPhone or other gadget. They manage to endure without any effort, because something – i.e. the cool tech device they want – overrides all discomfort and inconvenience.

Many years ago I tried to read a page of one of my brother's law books, a book on tort or property law. I found I had to keep rereading it, as I couldn't understand the convoluted message. I found myself resenting the book, thinking that having to read it in full would, for me, be tantamount to torture. It would take a great deal of money to persuade me to try to get through it. In contrast, if I look at some of my favourite books, it's actually more of an effort for me to *stop* reading them. Sometimes late at night I know I should stop reading and get more sleep, but the book is just too interesting. I am fighting off sleep in order to pursue the book.

In all these examples, there is nothing we need to *do* as such to be motivated. Motivation flows naturally when we pursue something we value. That means all we have to do is change the things we currently don't value enough (but need to value) and we will have tapped into a huge inner force of motivation. This motivation, in turn, acts like a kind of resilience to help us cope with the price of the things we pursue.

Now you have the right attitude, you have already engaged tremendous reserves of resilience in the pursuit of your goal.

In case you are thinking that we aren't as *naturally* tough and resilient as our grandfathers and forefathers (and therefore we should give up trying to be like them), I would like you to know that you have the same natural potential reserves of incredible resilience as any of our ancestors throughout the ages. After all, we are all human beings. It's just whether we choose to access these resources or not.

Historically, one of the hardest, most brutal training regimes ever known was that experienced by young boys in ancient Sparta. From the age of seven onwards, boys were taken into a military training boot camp and subjected to no-holes-barred combat, competitive flogging endurance tests, live-or-die tests with exposure to the elements, and so forth. I suspect if we had a time machine, and transported you as a baby back to the time and culture, you would endure things you would never have believed you could in this day and age. In terms of endurance and resilience, you would probably be indistinguishable from any other Spartan child.

Intrinsic values

Getting your hands on enough money to buy shiny consumer goods, designer clothes or a fancy sports car may in itself be sufficient motivation for you to relentlessly pursue your goal for success. If it is, then you can skip this bit – but bear in mind that many rich, beautiful and famous people, who have achieved the pinnacle of what society has told them is the ultimate success (fame and fortune), still feel unsatisfied or depressed, and ache for something more in life.

If you yearn for something more than impressing others with the size of your income, then you need to think about motivating yourself by intrinsic values, i.e. by pursuing some kind of higher value. Pursuing something that is 'bigger than you' means aiming for some kind of ideal, some kind of higher truth about what you are interested in, and exploring its highest expression. Consider for a moment the soldiers who apply for the notoriously brutal SAS or Navy SEALS training. Any applicant knows full well that they are entering a hellish selection and training process, with slim chance of success. Even if they make it to the end of this gruelling path, the job itself requires them to go and risk their lives, in the face of being maimed, tortured or killed. I'm pretty sure none of these Special Forces guys do it for the money (I don't think the money is that great in any case). They do it because they see membership of these elite units as the highest expression of military development.

In an even more straightforward example, very famous actors like Dame Judi Dench often carry on acting well into their golden years and long after they need the financial rewards. They find intrinsic satisfaction in perfecting their skills.

I'm a great fan of the TV show *Secret Millionaire*, about wealthy businessmen and women who go undercover in poor areas in order to find deserving organisations they would like to donate to. I'm continually in awe of the people who work in these organisations. They are usually unpaid volunteers who endure all sorts of trials to keep their charities and organisations running, living under the constant threat of bankruptcy. All these organisers are driven by a common value – to offer some sort of service to people in need. I very much doubt these people could be as driven if they just wanted a job for the money.

If you are not quite so idealistic, then how can you apply this principal more modestly in your working life? You might adopt a personal quest to be the best person you can be in your chosen field. This does not necessarily mean having to be the best in your company (as that is often driven by ego and the desire to be top dog, rather than pursuing the ideal). It is about competing with yourself, rather than others.

Recently I was becoming unsatisfied with the person who was cleaning my clinic. I don't think her heart was in it any more, or perhaps it never was. As soon as she arrived, she would go into autopilot, cleaning things that didn't need to be cleaned, and not cleaning other things that did need it. I was exasperated until a friend of mine recommended Aline, their own cleaner, who charged nearly double the rate. I tried Aline and noticed that she actually cared about the place looking clean. She would assess what needed the most attention and act accordingly. Occasionally she stayed 5–10 minutes over in order to finish something she was cleaning. It seemed to me that her goal was not clock-watching or doing the minimum possible. She was pursuing the ideal of a clean and orderly environment, and took satisfaction in converting chaos to order.

Obviously I am delighted with her work. I would pay her three times what she asking for if she wanted, and I plan to give her a big Christmas bonus. Not only is she getting more job satisfaction, but all her clients, just like me, tend to be delighted with her service and she is reaping the financial rewards by getting paid far more than her competitors.

Speaking for myself, I love my job. I would do my job even if I won the lottery and never had to work again. One of the many things I love about my job is that is allows me to pursue a 'truth' that is far bigger than me. I can constantly search for an understanding of how the human mind works, and never reach its limits. It's pretty impossible to get bored with something that never fails to challenge and surprise you, and keeps you growing. I'm also very interested in using hypnosis for therapy. I've had some great success with it in unexpected ways and am always interested in experimenting more to find out: *What are the limits of what I can do with hypnosis?* Note that this is about wanting to know *my* limits, how far can *I* go with it, rather than competing with others. I want to be the most effective person I can be using hypnosis. Competing against yourself to find your personal limits is a quest for personal development. Anything that makes you grow as a person is intrinsically rewarding; that's what makes it so fun.

Needless to say, when all these intrinsic values are being expressed in my job, it's very easy to be resilient when it comes to the less desirable aspects of my job (admin, accounts, marketing, etc) because the benefits I experience overpower the more undesirable aspects involved in my work. I could never have sustained the level of enthusiasm I have for my job for the money alone. Money is a by-product of my efforts, not the driving force.

As a bonus, if you enjoy your chosen field and engage with it, you will be constantly adding to and developing your skills. When you are regularly updating your skills then it is likely you will end up becoming very good at what you do. And the better you become at your job, the greater the personal sense of pride of achievement, recognition and financial reward you will experience.

The unsatisfied lawyer

I was once having a conversation with man in his mid-thirties, who works as a corporate lawyer in a well-known organisation. I'll call him Donald. Donald is good at his job even though at heart he would rather be a musician. If he won the lottery, he would quit his job in an instant.

He mentioned to me that he wasn't really satisfied with his job and felt a bit down. I asked Donald why, if he felt so down about it, he didn't quit his job? I mean, he was an adult with the right to make his own choices, and no one had a gun to his head. He replied that he couldn't quit because of the money.

As Donald said this, I remembered a similar conversation coming up between top performance coach Anthony Robbins and another man. Borrowing a leaf from Tony's book, I teased Donald, 'C'mon, no one actually works for pieces of paper with deceased notables on them. What is it about getting the money that keeps you in the job?'

'Well, with that money I get to have a good standard of living. I have my own house, eat well, and also get to send my daughter to private school.'

'And having a good standard of living and getting to send your daughter to private school … is that of value to you?'

'Yes,' he said, his eyes lighting up a bit. 'I want the best for her.'

'And what else is important to you about having a good standard of living?'

Donald started to recount how he liked going on two or three holidays a year, how he was able to buy some things that brought him pleasure, and so on.

I asked Donald what else he valued about his job. He replied quite quickly, 'The status.'

'And what is it about the status of your job that you value?'

'Well,' be began, clearly warming to the subject, then proceeded to reel off a list of other benefits – he liked having his own office; he liked having his own PA; he liked the medical benefits.

'So let me get this straight,' I said, when he was done. 'While you don't value your job as a lawyer in and of itself, you appreciate the fact that it allows you to have a standard of living that you *do* value, and provide the things that you and your family want? So would it be safe to say that you don't value your job directly, but indirectly?' Donald thought about it for a moment, then agreed that yes, this was the case.

Once a connection of value is made in one area, it is quite easy for that connection to be generalised to other areas. For example, indirect appreciation of your job can very easily spread to direct appreciation. In this case, Donald went away with an almost visible spring in his step.

Please note that at other times I have advised people that their best interests would be served by getting another job. I didn't view Donald as a man who was fundamentally unhappy in his job, but as someone who had lost appreciation for it, so that was the path I explored. The underlying point though is that, with a simple shift in attitude, Donald experienced the same job in a quite different way. He didn't have to leave his job or give up all the benefits it came with; he just needed to change his attitude.

In summary

> There are good attitudes (which move you towards your goals) and bad attitudes (which move you away from your goals).

> Your attitude needs to fit your desired goal if you want success.

> The 'right' attitude consists of:
- Knowing what you want
- Knowing the price for what you want
- Agreeing to pay the price.

> If you know what you want, know the price you need to pay and are prepared to pay it, you will engage and mobilise tremendous internal resources of motivation, endurance and resilience.

> Motivation and resilience are strongest when applied in pursuit of a higher value – a greater purpose, truth of the highest expression in your field.

> Despite activating these reserves, you may still not achieve your desired goal if there are additional pitfalls that may sabotage and derail your focus or desire. The rest of this book is devoted to addressing these pitfalls.

CHAPTER EXERCISE – ATTITUDE

1. Find a nice comfortable chair. Ensure you will not be disturbed for five minutes.

2. Imagine there is a magical bridge over time and time is no barrier. This bridge faces in the direction of the future.

3. The future it points to is one in which you are healthy, happy and in balance with your life.

4. Go out over this bridge for as many years as you feel are necessary for you to have arrived at your goal.

5. Go and observe your 'future self'. See what he or she is up to. What are they doing on a daily level that allows them to enjoy life?

6. Get a sense of *what* they are doing and *why* they are doing it (i.e. the benefits you feel by doing, having or being with those things).

7. Now you have some clarity on *what* you want (and *why* you want it), ask yourself if you are willing to pay the price for what you want.

8. If you are, imagine your decision is like a laser-guided tracking system that is locked onto your goal.

9. Once you are locked onto your goal, you have harnessed the power of your intent to unlock your reserves. Imagine your motivation and resilience is as powerful as the equivalent of a super-powerful missile in your arsenal, which has now been unleashed to pursue your goal.

10. Feel your determination and commitment welling up inside and being channelled toward your goal.

11. If you are not clear about your goal yet, don't worry and be patient. Decisions will come as more information presents itself to you. Even a rough outline of some things you would like to see in your future will be a start in defining your goals.

CHAPTER 2:
PERSONAL RESPONSIBILITY

People are always blaming their circumstances for what they are. I don't believe in circumstances. The people who get on in this world are the people who get up and look for the circumstances they want, and if they can't find them, make them.

– George Bernard Shaw

Personal responsibility as it relates to your goals for success in life should follow naturally when you have adopted the appropriate attitude and are following the directions mentioned in the previous chapter. However, it is such a vital and key component for career success, as well as success in your relationships and your overall psychological wellbeing, that it really merits its own chapter for more detailed exploration.

What is personal responsibility?

Personal responsibility is literally our 'response-ability' to things happening around us. When I think of my response-abilities, I imagine a quiver of options and tools (the arrows), which are available for me to respond to demands and challenges. If my quiver is well-stocked, I will be able to respond to the demands at hand quickly and efficiently to neutralise the problem (by firing my arrows at it). If my quiver is badly stocked and equipped, or I feel someone else is in charge of it, then I will respond poorly to the demands at hand.

A sense of personal responsibility ranges across a broad scale, from people who feel overly responsible for everyone and everything, to people who don't believe they are responsible for anything in their lives. Note that it's also possible to be very responsible in some areas of our lives, while being completely blinded to our responsibilities in other areas.

Personal responsibility is about balance.

Let's imagine that Bob and Mary have a minor disagreement. In scenario A, Mary tells Bob she is 'devastated' by Bob's disagreement and is extremely hurt. Bob reacts by feeling guilty and responsible for 'causing' Mary to be devastated. Bob continues to apologise profusely in order to make amends.

In scenario B, Bob and Mary have a more heated argument, and Bob starts swearing at Mary and acting in an aggressive manner. Mary objects to Bob's aggressive manner, but Bob completely excuses his behaviour because Mary 'made' him react that way. He feels he is reacting normally and Mary is out of order.

At times, people can say provocative things. At other times, they say neutral things, but we can react as if they are provocative. *The reaction we give is up to us.*

A healthy approach to personal responsibility is one in which you can put aside your own ego (your need to win, defend or justify your behaviour at all costs) and examine the higher 'truth' behind your interactions. Ask 'What is my own role and contribution in this interaction?' and 'What is the contribution and responsibility of the other person or parties involved?'

It's best to consider interactions with other people and your environment in terms of a system, where each element of the system influences and stimulates other elements. You are a part of any system of interaction with another person.

The degeneration of personal responsibility

It seems a general trend in the last thirty or forty years has seen government regulatory bodies, law courts, health services and other organisations shift the onus of responsibility away from individuals. As always, the intent and motives are well meaning, but the consequences have been counter-productive. Rather than helping society, teaching people that outside authorities are responsible for their health, behaviour and feelings has made society psychologically sicker.

Taking personal responsibility away from people tends to infantilise them, and delays their progress toward becoming healthy, autonomous, self-determining and resilient adults. Instead, policies that undermine individual responsibility create overgrown children who sulk or have temper tantrums when they don't get things their way.

When I worked in the NHS, I would routinely see people who thought that responsibility for their health was their doctor's problem. It was as if they thought it was *their* job to party (smoke excessively, eat the wrong food in the wrong quantity, drink excessively, take illicit drugs, fail to exercise, etc), and their doctor's job to look after their body and pick up the pieces afterwards. If these patients continued to suffer ill health from their activities, then the doctor really needed to try harder and make a more convincing case for change, or offer up a magic pill that would make everything better, without requiring any effort on the part of the patient!

In fairness to these clueless patients, drug companies and colluding doctors promote the idea that pills can be the answer to all our problems. The message being spread is, 'Why bother to help yourself when we will do it for you?'

In the courts, some types of lawyers have encouraged and indulged a culture of 'complain and blame', and patronising judges have agreed with such interpretations. This means that if I interpret something in an offensive way, others are to blame for the way I have interpreted and reacted, and I should be compensated. This has promoted a professional victim mentality that is not doing anyone any favours.

Granted that there are always some circumstances in which it's very clear that speech is offensive, e.g. hate speech, racial slurs, or speech that incites violence. These represent the more extreme ends of any 'bell curve' of communication, and there would be near-universal agreement about their offensiveness. I am referring more to comments that are otherwise neutral (the inverted 'U' part of the bell curve), which some people will choose to interpret as if they are at the extreme end of the scale.

In my consulting room, I see similar things happening, without the legal element. Some people have chosen, or have been trained, to make others responsible for their feelings and attributions. Change is impossible in these cases unless they are willing to take personal responsibility for their role in and contribution to the problems in their lives.

In general, I see two kinds of patients: blamers and doers. While it's true some problems are 'quick fixes' and some people are already equipped with the tools they need to deal with an issue, other problems will require a patient to develop a new skill or a quality. They will often need to embark on a process of personal development, to foster empathy for another's perspective, experiment with alternative forms of communicating, and consider different ways to understand people's reactions.

In such cases, a doer will come to me and say 'I have a problem. What can I do to fix it and free myself from this problem?' They will tackle proposed solutions with enthusiasm and will be appreciative and grateful throughout the process to boot.

A blamer will come to me and complain about their life. They are not interested in the large arsenal of techniques I am able to offer them for coping and responding better, because *they* don't want to change the problem. They want *me* to change the problem. They don't see therapy as engaging in a process of self-development. They get bored or restless if I describe tried-and-tested techniques to which doers will sit and listen with rapt attention. Blamers don't want to do any reading I might suggest, let alone apply the information that is capable of changing their lives. Much like the analogy I gave earlier of doctors who deal with hard-living patients, they see it as my job to take away the distress; it's their job to passively sit there, receive my help and complain if it's not working.

I sometimes make the equivalent analogy of going to a personal trainer and saying, 'Make me lose weight.' When he replies, 'Alright, every day you need to do 30 sit-ups and 20 push-ups,' I don't look at him in amazement and say, 'Oh, I don't want to do that. That's boring and painful. Can't you do them for me?'

As mentioned earlier, we may display great personal responsibility in some areas of our lives, but not in others. This may be due to ignorance (arising from a genuine conceptual blind spot) about our role in things. Other times it's just because of habit, or because we have not 'grown up' in that area. Maturing and growing up is the antidote to a lack of personal responsibility.

We are meant to develop into mature and responsible adults, but our efforts can be thwarted by the influence of the following sources of information. Any source or organisation that seeks to promote a culture of blame and complain will be at odds with the development of personal responsibility.

To free yourself from this propaganda and indoctrination, we need to examine these sources' credibility and realise there are alternative ways of looking at and interpreting things than they profess.

Ready to be de-programmed from these institutions' typical doctrine? Then let's begin.

Sources that diffuse personal responsibility

Parents and family

One of the major reasons we may fail to take enough personal responsibility in our lives is simple – it's due to pure habit.

When we are born, one or more of our parents are completely responsible for all our needs. If we experience an unmet need, our job is to scream and cry to communicate our distress, and it's our parents' job to figure out what we are distressed about. As far as we are concerned, our job is to keep screaming at them until they get it right.

As we grow older and learn to point, and then speak, we make it a bit easier for them by giving them clues here and there, but as far as we are concerned, we are still in effect the 'talent' and they are the 'agents' who take care of all our needs. If we want a toy, our job is to nag Mummy or Daddy until one of them caves in. It's not our problem whether our parents can afford more toys for us, whether there is room for more toys, or whether we will grow bored of the toy within a few days. Our job is simply to want things and it's their job to keep us in supply.

Now, as can be guessed, some people are better at growing out of these habits than others. As we get older, we might say to our mother, 'Mum, I'm hungry', and this time, instead of jumping into action, she rolls her eyes and say, 'Felix, you've got a pair of working arms and legs haven't you? You've got a functional brain? You want to be a grown-up, don't you? Why don't you go over to the fridge and make yourself a sandwich?' In this case, it might dawn on me that I do indeed possess the capability to make myself a snack. I do exactly that and, hey presto, I can now meet my own need for sandwiches. As long as I have the ingredients for sandwiches in the fridge, I will never go hungry wherever I am. Moreover, I might even become rather proud of having made my own sandwich. I did it all by myself.

Pleased with my success, I start to get daring, experimenting with other ingredients. In fact, it's come to the point where I've started showing off my new sandwich-making skill to others. One day, when Mum comes in, I seize my opportunity and say, 'Hungry, Mum? Here, why don't you put your feet up and let me make you a sandwich?' My mum is grateful and I feel very pleased with myself. Score: win-win. We are all pleased with how things turned out.

All well and good. But imagine, in scenario B, that when my mother tells me to make my own sandwich, I object. My internal system doesn't like this new change, this new requirement to expend energy when I am all comfortable watching sports on TV. I give my mum a guilt trip, or threaten to eat nothing, or claim helplessness. In this case, Mum gives up, pulls up her sleeves and takes over to make me my sandwich. Score: 'win' for me. I congratulate myself for escaping an important lesson.

Even worse, imagine scenario C. I yell 'Hungry!' to Mum. She jumps up and fusses about me without any attempt at getting me to make my own sandwich. I grow up thinking this is totally appropriate and part of the natural order of things. As far as I am concerned, when I have a need, it's someone else's duty to meet it, not mine. In fact if they don't do their 'job' properly (their job being to make me happy), I get furious at them for being so lax and lazy and bad at their jobs. If they attempt to insert their own needs somewhere into the equation, I am even more angry. How dare they? Don't they realise I am the centre of the universe and they are just my satellites. And that by trying to factor their own needs in, they are violating the very laws of nature? I might even get angry at them for not anticipating my needs, so I don't have to suffer the discomfort of explaining them.

My parents, eager to pacify or please me, apologise, grovel and make amends. Score: 'win' for parents, or so they think. They believe they have successfully catered to all my whims and desires, not realising they are manufacturing a little tyrant.

As you can see, over-protective and people-pleasing parents can essentially de-skill a child and teach it to make others responsible for its needs. At all costs, you must hang on to your sense of personal responsibility. Don't let your parents or well-meaning family members try and take this 'burden' off you.

If you recognise yourself in scenario C, have been treated like the centre of the universe and expect others to cater to all your whims, then know that this is usually a path to disaster. You have been taught some very unhelpful ideas about how the world works. As time goes on, you will alienate your partner, colleagues and everyone else around you, ending up angry, bitter and alone. The earlier you have a reality-check about this, the better. Re-create your internal universe and reposition yourself as one of the many planets that orbits the Sun (a higher truth), rather than thinking you are the centre of it.

Even if a child has tried to fend off its over-protective parents, he will likely still face other sources who are trying to teach it the same unhelpful lessons.

Society at large – language

Society is comprised of individuals. Individuals in turn interpret the world around them in certain ways and attribute 'causes' to most events. If enough individuals are in agreement about how something has been caused, then this will be reflected in their common language.

Language gives us clues about how different societies interpret cause and effect. For instance, some cultures will attribute the behaviour of a mentally ill person to possession by a malevolent spirit. Others conclude that events happen because it is the 'will of God'.

In Western societies, we have historically placed a high value on rationalism, which has promoted a certain linear thinking style. This manner of thinking considers things in terms of 'event A precedes event B' (in a factory, for example, 'the problem was caused by the screw coming loose in the cam shaft').

This linear thinking style is sufficient for the less complex, static mechanical systems involved in manufacturing, but is woefully inadequate when applied to dynamic, paradoxical, multi-level systems – like human beings.

When the formula of 'event A precedes event B' is used to try to understand human communication and behaviour, it can lead to overly simplistic interpretations of that behaviour, such as a misguided sense that we 'know' A *caused* B.

Consider, for instance, the observer of an argument saying something like, 'His criticism *caused* her to feel hurt.' They have understood the interaction as follows:

> Observer sees A giving feedback to B.
> B reacts by feeling hurt.
> If B is hurt, it must then follow, using this formula, that what *caused* the sadness must have been the feedback (which preceded B).
> If the feedback caused the hurt, then it must have been *intended* to cause the hurt.
> The feedback is now seen only as *hurtful criticism*.

This line of thinking ends up making A wholly responsible for all effects present, taking away any personal responsibility from B for her reaction. It is seen only in terms of his criticism being *intended* to put her down and make her unhappy This interpretation ignores all other possibilities. For example, maybe the feedback was necessary and appropriate, and phrased in neutral language, but B interpreted it in terms of, 'Why don't you like me? Why are you picking on me?' Her reaction may have had nothing to do with the message actually being communicated.

If A's actions caused B's reactions, and we therefore assume that A *intended* the occurrence of B, we move onto the subject of moral judgements such as, 'What he does is bad, therefore he must be a malicious person.' With enough experience interpreting things in this way, we end up skipping straight to the moral judgements: 'You criticised me and made me feel bad because you are mean and a bad person.' This makes the interpreter feel like a blameless victim who is simply being picked on. If law courts agree with you, then this type of faulty attribution becomes enshrined and enforced in law, which further legitimises this method of interpreting events.

We love finding simple linear 'causes'. Newspapers love to reassure us that we know the cause of inexplicable behaviour, summing it up in simple conclusions, such as 'He was a monster', or stating that widespread city riots that occurred in the UK in 2011 were caused by a small band of 'bad' ringleaders, when it seems more likely that there were myriad reasons for the way things turned out.

In fact, the very reason there are so many 'blamers' in our culture is precisely due to our preoccupation with causes. We want to know who 'caused' something to happen so we can apportion righteous blame and excuse ourselves from any deeper thinking about the issue.

Back to language. When an individual experiences something and wants to make sense of it, they choose the language with which they describe it. The very language *available to them* will influence the individual to ascribe meaning to his or her experience in a certain way, which often puts responsibility on others for 'causing' their distress. So sometimes even our vocabulary is set against us taking more responsibility in our lives! We have to start using more neutral language, which allows for multiple possible causes, and less suggestive language.

Society at large – institutions

Society and its laws can act as a kind of over-protective parent.

If lawmakers behave like over-protective, patronising parents, who encourage people to lay the blame for problems at other people's feet, this prevents citizens from taking ownership of their behaviour and cultivating personal responsibility. Laws that are formed in this spirit send a strong message that others are the cause of all our distress, regardless of our personal interpretations.

As such, we have seen a seeming endless litany of cases in the media in which people are seeking compensation for their own hurt feelings, distress or irresponsible behaviour. In other parts of the world, it's your own damn fault if you buy a hot coffee and spill it on yourself. You asked for hot coffee and were given hot coffee in a functional cup that millions of others use daily. But in the Western world we've seen high-profile cases of people getting a little drunk, climbing out of windows onto roofs, walking where they are not meant to be walking, falling and hurting themselves and then trying to sue the owners of the property on which they've trespassed because they did not have sufficient 'safety' precautions in place to save these people from their own stupidity. Apparently some people feel they need to be explicitly warned and protected from climbing onto roofs, suggesting that walking on roofs is a reasonable thing to do unless someone expressly informs them otherwise; their behaviour is due to the failure of others to get this message across.

There are now messages on packets of peanuts – containing *just* peanuts – warning people not to eat peanuts if they are allergic to them. Presumably the manufacturers are trying to protect those zombie-like consumers who are allergic to peanuts but will still buy a packet without taking any responsibility for *knowing* what they have bought, even when all the obvious evidence would suggest that, if they open the packet, they are likely to encounter peanuts. Peanut manufacturers likely feel compelled to include these messages, to avoid the inevitable lawsuits that would follow if they did not. Has it really come to this? At this point in our evolution, do we really need to protect people from even the minimum amount of rational thinking they might apply in considering the consequences of their actions?

Laws influence every other institution, because of course no one wants to get sued. So schools would rather prevent pupils from any sort of experience that could result in a freak accident (e.g. playing conkers), however remotely unlikely it might be. In this culture of fear, the message is being clearly sent: 'We are all afraid that you will blame us for any mishap because, of course, you can.'

If we are part of a game, but we do not know we are participants in a game, then we will continue to be played. But once we know we are involved in a game, then we have a choice as to whether we want to continue being part of this game or not. Now that you know that you are part of a 'game' played by society – a widespread blame game – you have the power to be *irreverent* about these influences.

You can choose an alternative interpretation other than the one society would like you to buy into. In so doing, you will have freed up some mental space, and made room for other healthier choices and options to go in its place. What I suggest you fill that space with instead are notions of responsibility that you have examined, agreed with and chosen. Here are some suggestions.

The building blocks of personal responsibility
The creator position
The first and most important building block for responsibility is better understanding cause and effect.

I am now going to ask you to consider the concept of 'cause and effect' in an unusual way. I realise that at the start of this chapter I made it clear that responsibility lies on a continuum, and that it's wise to know what is and isn't our responsibility – otherwise we will start being overly responsible for others.

What I am going to propose is meant in a different spirit. Even though I already *know* that everything that happens in your life is not your responsibility, I am going to suggest that *you act as if it is.*

Why? Because pretending you are responsible for everything in a given situation allows you to react in different ways. It's a bit like expecting you will have to do a task on your own, and then being pleasantly surprised when unexpected assistance becomes present – preparing to move some heavy boxes all on your own when out of nowhere a friend pops in and offers to help out.

In this spirit of looking at things differently, I would like you to imagine that when anything happens in your life, you can respond in one of two ways: you can either be *at cause* with what happened or *at effect* with what happened.

Being 'at effect' involves adopting either a passive 'victim' position or child-like position. Things are done unto us and we don't like them. We feel hard done by and we react with complaint, blame or self-pity. Being 'at effect' is very disempowering because we act as if others have the power. We place ourselves into a subservient 'one-down' position. We blame others or God or life or fate for all our circumstances. We also feel envious and jealous of others who do not have our bad misfortune.

When we focus on these things, it means we are not focusing on other more useful things, such as our choices and options – our 'response-abilities'.

In contrast, being 'at cause' is an empowering position in which we are the authors of our lives and circumstances. We feel more powerful and resilient because we know that we always have an input and a say in things. We are active stake-holders in our lives and happiness.

In order to be 'at cause', you will need to pretend to be the sole 'creator' of your universe. In order to do so, imagine this: *Suppose I am the creator of my universe and responsible for all the creations in my universe, including all my problems. If I am not happy with my universe, what am I doing or not doing that's allowing these problems to be present?*

Try it. If you act as a creator, rather than a victim, you will always feel more powerful and aware of your choices and your ability to influence things, and more like you have a say in your fate and happiness. It stands to reason that putting yourself in the position of a god is going to make you feel more powerful than putting yourself in the position of a mere mortal (though do stop short of developing a god-complex, which is never advisable!).

In times of duress, ask yourself 'Am I in a creator position or a subject position?' If you realise you are in the 'subject' position, switch sides and go over to the creator position by asking yourself the question above. Then do what you need to do until you feel you are addressing your unresolved problem, i.e. until you are 'at cause' with it.

I remember once explaining this concept to a patient of mine who immediately replied with, 'But yes, that's what I do. When people don't respond the way I want, I immediately think, "What's wrong with me, what have I done wrong?"' This is not the creator position. The creator position would respond in a different spirit:

Creator: What am I doing/not doing that's allowing these problems to still exist?
Reply: I need to learn how to overcome my social anxiety and speak with confidence.
Creator: What am I doing/not doing that's allowing my block of social anxiety and speaking with confidence to still exist?
Reply: I'm not learning how to overcome these problems.
Creator: What am I doing/not doing that's allowing me to not learn how to overcome these problems?
Reply: I need to get the right information.
Creator: What am I doing/not doing that's allowing me to not have the right information?
Reply: Oh, I need to find someone or something that has the right information.

Creator: Good, now you're at cause. Go forth and find someone appropriate, and then we'll take it from there.

The case of Eli

Eli was a young woman in her mid-twenties, a counselling psychology trainee doing her masters at my old university. I was acting as her supervisor at the time. One day Eli came to our session with a long face. I asked her what was up and she replied gloomily that she had submitted her proposal for a thesis to the ethics board two months before, and they hadn't approved it yet. Now she was worrying about running out of time to start (and subsequently finish) her dissertation. If the board did not approve the title soon, she needed to know so she could come up with another title, or at the very least stop hanging around waiting.

Now on the face of it, this situation would appear to be out of her hands. How can you argue with a faceless board of examiners?

The answer is quite easily if you adopt the creator position.

After guiding Eli through the concept, I asked her to imagine what options and possibilities she could pursue. I asked her to imagine that she was among 'equals' and had a say in the processing of her proposed title. We brainstormed and role-played how to overcome the usual objections. I also suggested that bureaucratic organisations tend be risk-aversive and motivated by pain. We are designed to pursue pleasure and avoid pain. If work is tedious or uncertain (as in, no one wants to take the risk of approving a dissertation experiment that could lead to unforeseen risks and come back to haunt you), then the reviewer will have some associated some degree of 'pain' with doing their work. The pain and uncertainty means they will drag their heels over it and have to force themselves to do it. The pain of doing the work therefore needs to be greater than the pain of not doing it. Eli needed to create for them the experience of more pain for not approving her title, than would be caused by reviewing her title and making a decision. Her conviction in pursuing her cause had to be greater than their conviction in avoiding work.

Eli smiled with pleasure at the thought of getting her own back by being a bit of a nuisance. A condensed version of her response went something like this:

[*Eli rings ethics board*]

Eli: I'd like to speak to the specific person in charge of approving my proposed dissertation. Could you tell me who that is please?

Reception: I don't know [*expecting the conversation to end there*].

Eli: That's OK, can you tell me who would know?

Reception: [*surprised and a little taken aback*] Erm, well I think it would be the manger Mr Smith … but he's not in right now. [*said with a triumphant expectation of regaining power*]

Eli: No problem, can you tell me when he will be back so I can visit him?

Reception: Oh, erm, I'm not sure. Sometime today.

Eli: When do you think you will have an idea?

Reception: Err… maybe after 2pm?

Eli: Great. I will be there at 2pm and wait for him.

Reception: [*not wanting a nagging student hanging around the waiting room*] 'OK, hold on, I'll just go and find out exactly what time he will be back.'

[*Mr Smith calls Ellie back*]

Eli: Hello Mr Smith. I see that my title has not been approved yet. Can you tell me what the specific hold-up is, please, so I can help?

Mr Smith: Oh, no hold-up as such. Nothing you need to help with.

Eli: Then there is no reason for the delay. So when do you estimate you *will* review it?

Mr Smith: Err, by Thursday?

Eli: Great, I will call you on Thursday. What time would that be exactly?

Mr Smith: [*beginning to realise this problem won't go away, and sighing*] I will look at if first thing and call you tomorrow at noon.

Eli's resilience and 'creator' attitude paid off. She got her approval within the week.

Don't take things personally

Obviously there are times when people do or say things with the intent of putting you down. I am not talking about these times. I am talking of innocent neutral comments, which some people take personally.

Taking neutral comments to heart is about interpreting other people's remarks based on your own insecurities and baggage. In order to take things to heart, you must only allow for one interpretation and ignore all other possible interpretations. Taking something to heart also disregards the fact that YOU are responsible for your interpretations.

Blaming is a form of expressing, 'I am hurt, you are responsible for my interpretation, you should feel bad.'

In order to stop taking things personally, it is vital to understand that multiple frames of interpretation exist, of which yours is just one among many. As such, when someone says something to which your first instinct is to take offence, it's best to:

> Clarify what the other person actually means and intends before jumping to conclusions.[3]

> Understand the person on *their* terms rather than yours. You are not the centre of their universe. They may not know your universe well at all. They do know their own universe, and that is where they are coming from.

> If someone has offended you, it may have nothing to do with intent and everything to do with a cultural misunderstanding.

By 'culture' I don't just mean different ethnic cultures, but the different cultures experienced by men and women, by different generations, by different religious and political affiliations, and so on. With all of these relative variables bouncing around and interacting, of course there is going to be some ignorance and misunderstanding. When this happens, don't take it personally and get on your high horse, convinced that you have been victimised. Do some detective work first and clarify the spirit of the points being made as the other person understands them.

Remember, announcing 'I'm offended' is basically telling the world that you can't control your own interpretations and emotions, so everyone else should do it for you.

I believe most cases of political correctness reflect an imbalance in Western society, with some individuals taking little or no responsibility for their interpretation or contribution, and other individuals taking too much responsibility, rushing to appease and placate the offended parties. In so doing, the overly responsible members unwittingly disempower the offended members, offering no incentive for change, growth and maturity.

Imagine a teacher giving a child a justified low mark for poor performance, the child having a tantrum and a parent rushing to give

3. As I come across ambiguous information, I try to remind myself to 'clarify, clarify, clarify'. Clarification is to good communication what 'location, location, location' is to property.

the teacher a piece of his mind because the child was offended by the low mark. What message and effect would that have on the child? It would only serve to reinforce and legitimise this behaviour, keeping the child stuck in this immature phase.

Ownership

Ownership is a sign of maturity. In this case, it refers to taking ownership of your responsibilities and needs. As a child, it is someone else's job to understand and discern your needs while you passively wait for them to get it right or wrong. As an adult you are responsible for understanding and meeting your physical and emotional needs.

The familiar passage from the book of Corinthians in the Bible is a timely reminder here: *When I was a child, I spoke as a child, I understood as a child, I thought as a child: but when I became a man, I put away childish things.* [4]

It's time to put away childish habits and be an adult. As an adult, ask yourself 'What do *I* want and what do *I* need?'

For instance, if you are bored, you can now put yourself in the creator position and be 'at cause' with your needs by asking yourself, 'What am I doing/not doing that's allowing this boredom to still exist?'

Suppose part of you replies, 'I need stimulation.' Continuing to be 'at cause' means you continue to ask, 'What kind of stimulation? Physical, sporting, reading, walking, talking, shopping, something creative?' Keep asking until you have a sense of the real underlying need, rather than depending on someone else to mind-read or second-guess you. That is no longer age-appropriate for an adult. The same process can be applied to every other area of your life: work, relationships, health, and so on.

---

4. King James Bible, 13:11.

Taking ownership for your safety: builders

The culture of complain and blame, allied to the subsequent fear of litigation, has created a Big Brother health and safety nightmare that interferes with progress. For instance, a friend of mine, Gillian, told me that she had some builders working in her garden. One of them wanted to come in the house and use the toilet. Not having a downstairs toilet at the time, and just having laid brand new carpets on the stairs and upper floors, Gillian saw the builder's boots were muddy, and the following interaction occurred:

Gillian: Would you mind taking your boots off before going up the stairs?

Builder: We're not allowed to do that. H&S regulations say I could slip without shoes on.

Alright, Gillian thought. Apparently it's OK for your children to go upstairs in their socks, but not grown men.

Gillian: Well, you're not going to wreck my new carpet. How about you borrow my husband's slippers?

Builder: I can't, H&S says we need to keep our shoes on.

After a bit of back and forth, the builder agreed to put plastic bags over his shoes, because there were no regulations against that. Correct me if I'm wrong, but I suspect plastic bags on shoes would be a lot more slippery than socks!

The builder completely gave up ownership of his responsibility to climb the stairs with due care, instead handing responsibility over to H&S policies, which might not always make sense. In contrast, Gillian soon after had a Polish builder in, doing some work on the basement. This time, when the builder asked to use the toilet and Gillian indicated it was upstairs, he slipped off his shoes unprompted. The latter builder took ownership of his own responsibility for due care.

In terms of ownership of your *communication*, at the start of this chapter I gave an example to illustrate that problem with a simple linear cause and effect style. In this earlier example, in which 'his criticism caused her hurt', I used the scenario of a person feeling hurt because she may have interpreted the communication as more critical than it actually was.

It is of course also possible that the person who was giving the feedback did also communicate the information in a demeaning or disparaging way, using a certain tone, inflection, facial expression or choice of negative words. In this case, the communicator also needs to be aware of their own responsibility in how they deliver information. Of course, perhaps the communicator was reacting to an earlier past history of poor performance and was less patient than he usually would be. Or perhaps he is easily frustrated, has perfectionistic tendencies and didn't communicate something adequately; this in turn could have resulted in the person being criticised not being able to do her job properly, leading to poor performance.

Either way, cause and effect is rarely ever a linear affair. Even if you don't feel responsible for something, it's worth taking a moment to consider that you just *might* be communicating in a way you are unaware of. A simple acknowledgement of your *potential* contribution usually does wonders to express respect to the other person and avoid needless hard feelings, or prevent a situation degenerating into an argument. I find a sentence such as, 'If I am raising my voice or switching to a different tone without being aware of it, I apologise. It was not my intention to act in an intimidating manner,' to be useful. Also try to remember to:

> Consider and respect the other person's point of view (e.g. if the other person says, 'Don't raise your voice at me.'). Even if you do not feel you are raising your voice, you might well be, without even knowing it.

> Accept the possibility of unwittingly doing something, and take ownership of it.

> Offer a 'conditional' apology in case you are responsible. A conditional apology is one that begins '*if* I am raising my voice, *then* I apologise'. You are not being made to apologise for something you haven't done. You are potentially apologising for something you may have done, and feeling good about taking personal responsibility.

Doer, Not Complainer

A doer focuses on results. A complainer focuses on 'reasons' rather than results.

Suppose I find myself at point A in my career or relationship. I realise I am no longer content with being at point A. I chew things over and decide I want to be at point B instead, because point B represents the things I aspire to be or have. I have now created a goal for myself.

Any time you decide you are unhappy at point A and decide to move to point B, you are acting like a doer, being responsible for on deciding a goal and then pursuing it.

Now, in contrast, suppose I am a point A again and I hate being at point A. All I know is that I don't like being at point A. I haven't taken any responsibility for clarifying what I want instead. In such a case, I would remain stuck at point A, focusing my energies on analysing the reasons why I am at point A in the first place, or figuring out who or what is to blame for holding me back.

Even if my 'goal' were just to get as far away from point A as possible, that would still mean there would be no point B, as such. There are an infinite number of directions away from point A, any of which could be a lot worse, and I might find myself complaining about them even more.

In the neat little book *The One Minute Manager*, a scenario is recounted in which an employee goes to his boss with a problem. The boss listens and says, 'If you can't tell me what you'd like to be happening, you don't have a problem yet. You're just complaining. A problem exists only if there is a difference between what is actually happening and what you desire to be happening.'

In other words, if I decide I no longer want to be at point A and want to move to point B, but there is an obstacle in the way that I truly do not know how to move, then I have a genuine bona fide, legitimate 'problem'. Having or experiencing problems is fine. It's natural. Life is a series of problems, which need to be solved in pursuit of our goals. There is a difference, though, between addressing a problem and complaining.

So in any situation you are not content with in your life, pause a moment and ask yourself: 'Do I have an actual problem or am I just complaining?'

If you have a genuine problem, keep working on how to resolve it. You are allowed to ask for guidance and advice to solve your problem.

If you are just complaining, then say to yourself, 'Well, either do something about it or stop complaining.'

If you make a stand and say 'I am responsible for my problem', then there is no room, no entry point for blame to be present. People who take responsibility do not blame. They are too busy considering how they will solve the problem to get then to the destination they want.

Duty

A duty is a moral or legal obligation, i.e. a responsibility. We all have duties to fulfil, whether they involve working in a salaried job, looking after children, or studying to pass exams. We also have a duty to grow up and accept the next stage in our life's development, e.g. from child to grown up, or from dependent to independent.

We have a choice in how we face our respective duties. We can try to shirk them, or we can make the best of them.

I find it helps to think about how we discharge our duties in terms of being professional or unprofessional.

A true professional, for instance, does not let personal issues interfere with their job. They do their job regardless of how tired they are, whatever else is going on in their life, no matter how they feel about their customers or clients, and they don't take other people's upsets personally.

Needless to say, non-professionals let all sorts of personal baggage interfere with their job, take things personally, and complain endlessly about the requirements of their work.

We've all had experiences of people who are professional and unprofessional in their jobs. Not only is it much nicer to be on the receiving end of professional service or conduct, it's also nicer for the professional themselves. Professionals enjoy their jobs more, because there is a real pleasure in knowing one is good at one's job. Others also notice this and may provide positive feedback. Consequently, professionals esteem and value their jobs and therefore themselves, because they acknowledge that they are good at doing the things they value.

Personally I also think that what helps make professionals professional is that they focus on a higher calling – perhaps the value they place on doing a job well – which allows them to be more resilient when faced with challenges.

If you are a parent, you are already probably more professional than you realise. It's likely that when your baby woke you up for the third time that night, that you got up and provided whatever she needed, regardless of how you felt. You probably didn't say, 'Well, what about me, I'm tired too.' You kept your own problems out of it. What enabled you to do this was your higher calling – the love for your child that swept all your personal considerations to the side.

You have this resource within you. The mechanism operating it can be channelled anywhere in your life where you want to apply it.

If faced with a duty, choose to be a professional and you will find yourself feeling more resilient, and getting more satisfaction from your job.

Face the music and admit mistakes

Once upon a time in my youth, I stumbled upon a great secret.

I had made a mistake of some kind. I can't even remember what it was about, but I was called to stand before the person to whom I was accountable. Again I can't remember if it was a teacher or a parent.

I was faced with a choice. I could try to deny, defend or talk my way out of what I did in an attempt to reduce or avoid punishment. Or I could be a 'man', so to speak, and face the music.

Since I genuinely felt remorseful about what I did, and thought punishment was appropriate, I did not try to lie or defend myself. I admitted the mistake I made and, since I had no excuses to offer, expected the full punishment to subsequently follow. To my surprise, the person I admitted fault to smiled, said something encouraging that I can't remember, and the next thing I knew I was outside the room without having been punished.

I thought for a moment that perhaps he had not understood that I had just fully confessed to my mistake. But it then dawned on me that the person was less interested in doling out punishment for its own sake than he was in getting me to understand the consequences of my actions, in order to make things better next time round.

So simple, really, but a big revelation at the time.

Next time I messed something up, I did the same thing and admitted my fault. I didn't know whether the first person was unduly lenient or not, but to my delight, I had a similar outcome. The injured party was again more merciful than vengeful.

In light of these experiences I concluded that if you have made a genuine mistake and deny or defend that mistake, you are more likely to face reprisals, either because the injured party doesn't believe you and wants to teach you a lesson, or by spending the next three hours arguing.

In fact, it seems what really gets people's goat is not making a mistake in the first place (because we all mess up from time to time), but when you refuse to accept any responsibility for your mistake. This sends the other person into a crusading frenzy in which they become hell-bent on showing you the error of your ways and proving to you what a lying, cheating, deceitful person you are.

If, on the other hand, you readily accept your mistake, are sincere and willing to make amends, suddenly everyone becomes lenient, magnanimous and merciful. They rarely want to carry out the full retribution or punishment that they are entitled to. The whole mistake usually becomes quickly sorted and filed, and everyone moves on. No one feels the need to teach you any necessary lessons, because you are demonstrating that you have already learnt your lesson.

If this formula for minimising fall-out is so easy, why isn't everyone doing it? I suspect many people are afraid of admitting any liability. In the business and corporate world, people are wary that any admission of liability could lead to litigation. And unfortunately, lawyers are often less interested in you learning your lesson than in parting you from your money.

In the private domain, people regularly confuse making a stupid mistake with being a stupid person. If someone makes an error of judgement, it does not mean that ALL their judgements are discredited and stupid. An intelligent person does not always have to act in intelligent ways. You can be an intelligent person, but do silly things daily. Just ask my wife.

It's a lot easier to admit stupid mistakes when you can firstly *accept this in yourself*: 'I am a smart person, but occasionally I will not do smart things. My smart decisions, though, greatly outweigh my errors.'

Secondly, it's a lot easier to admit stupid mistakes when you realise the music you have to face is usually not so bad anyway. I mean, if I admit a mistake to my teacher, what's the worst that will happen? He isn't going to flog me. If I admit a mistake to my boss, I rationally know she is not going to have the guards haul me away, put me in the stocks and have passersby throw rotten fruit at me. The very worst case scenario is that I look for another job – but my life is never going to be in mortal peril or even subject to physical pain.

If you admit a mistake to your parents, providing your parents are decent enough human beings, it's likely that they will only be miffed with you for a bit. Once you reach a certain size, even spanking is no longer a real threat.

In reality, when I look back at times I have made blunders, the worst that happened was that I would be in the dog house for a while. Some people would be a little bit fed up or disappointed in me about whatever mistake I made, and then they got over it, moved on, and probably will forget all about it down the line. I just had to lie low, ride out the necessary time, make amends, and everything would soon be made right again. It's hardly a sentence to hard labour in a Siberian gulag.

So, if you find that you have made a mistake, be a 'man' or 'woman', be a grown up about it, take responsibility, admit, apologise, and offer to make amends. Yes, you may have to go through a slightly awkward phase of not being in the offended parties' best books, but that too will pass and you will be back in their good graces in no time. In any case, it's likely they will be more lenient with you than they would otherwise, and they'll have more respect for you on another level.

In summary

> Personal responsibility refers to the range of options and choices we have when responding to the demands facing us.

> Some people fail to take *enough* responsibility for their contributions, while others take *too much* and become overly responsible for the feelings of others.

> It's possible to be responsible in some areas of your life and not in others.

> Taking personal responsibility where it is due will make you

mentally healthier and more resilient. Be honest when assessing what *is* and what is *not* your area of personal responsibility in any given interaction. You do this not to 'win' any argument, but because mental health is an ongoing commitment to the truth. If you are not committed to the truth, then you are in denial of reality and out of touch with reality.

> If your parents were overly protective, inadvertently teaching you that others are responsible for your welfare, your task is to free yourself from this training.

> Institutions in society seem to be indulging a culture of complaining and blaming others. This is an unhealthy indoctrination that we need to recognise and transcend by not subscribing to it.

> The 'creator position' is a useful perspective from which to review personal responsibility.

> Taking genuinely neutral comments to heart is about falsely interpreting other people's remarks due to your own insecurities and baggage.

> Blaming is a form of expressing: 'I am hurt and you are responsible for my interpretation. You should feel bad.'

> Ownership refers to owning your role in clarifying and meeting your physical, emotional and vocational needs and duties.

> When doing your duty, wear a professional hat. This will make your job more rewarding and satisfying, for yourself and others with whom you interact.

> Be a doer. If you are unhappy at point A, take responsibility for finding out where you would like to be at instead (point B), then pursue your new goal with perseverance to overcome obstacles in the way.

> If you make a mistake, be willing to face the music. You might be pleasantly surprised by people's reactions to your honesty and willingness to take responsibility for your actions.

CHAPTER EXERCISE – THE CHOICE

Of course it wouldn't be fitting to end a chapter about responsibility if you weren't given some kind of opportunity to be responsible for your choices.

> Imagine a choice of paths awaits you, a path to the left and a path to the right.

> The path to the left represents a life of complaining and blaming everyone else for your decisions, feelings and reactions, an endless loop of 'it's not my fault you made me feel x'.

> The path to the right represents growing up, taking personal responsibility and implementing the steps explained in this chapter.

> Turn and face the left path and imagine you could time travel down this virtual future for 10 or 20 years. Then pause and take notice of what your life is like here and how you feel about it. You will probably find that, on this path, you feel a background sense of discontent and bitterness towards others around you, for not acting the way you want them to be. You find yourself to be a moaner and a whiner. You find yourself surrounded only by people-pleasers you despise.

> Now rewind and go back to the fork in the road. Turn and face the path to the right. Experience travelling down the path to the right, for the same amount of time.

> Pause and take stock of how you feel here. You have grown up, you feel more in control and confident in your life. You have achieved more, you are mentally healthier and more robust, and you are also liked and respected more by the people around you. You are a better role model for your kids or the people around you in general. Notice everything about this virtual future life.

> Now rewind back to the beginning. A choice of paths awaits you.

> Would you rather be an immature, petty tyrant, more interested in getting your way, alienating others and with a permanent feeling of

being dissatisfied with the world around you? Or would you rather be a mature, healthy individual who feels proud about their growth, actions and behaviour, who commands the respect of those around them?

It's your choice.

CHAPTER 3: PERSEVERANCE

You miss 100% of the shots you don't aim for.

– Wayne Gretzky

Perseverance is persistence in a course of action, a purpose or a state, especially when faced with difficulties, obstacles, or discouragement.

Many, many successful people are NOT smarter than you or me. They are not even the most talented in their field (certain very successful but not very talented pop groups spring to mind).

The secret is that they:

- are *clear* about what they want, and then
- they *persevere* in getting what they want.

I'm not talking about scenarios in which, once you've made up your mind, you must stick with your decision regardless of what happens, and see everything through to the bitter end. That's just foolish. Sometimes decisions are incomplete or misguided. Sometimes a business idea is flawed and needs to be dropped. Sometimes the girl or boy you are hell-bent on wooing is just not interested in you, no matter how much you try to impress them. Persistence is not always a magic wand. Often we need to reappraise, adapt and be flexible.

I am talking about situations in which people quit too soon, giving up prematurely before they achieve the success that would have been available to them with just a little more patience and resilience.

I am talking about situations when you are very confident that the end goal will benefit you, and all that's in the way is a lot of hard work. This could apply to studying for a qualification that will raise your income, working your way up your career ladder, starting your own business with a viable plan, organising or decorating your house, writing a book or improving your physical fitness.

In these all cases, perseverance is an essential ingredient. And you need resilience in order to be persistent and pursue your goals.

Recently I was reading a book by an author who wrote that, 'Often we fail to reach our goal because we are not stubborn enough in our striving towards it. Many goals simply do not get the time to realise themselves, especially when you quickly grow cold towards your goal and give up on the "hopeless" case.'

The author then goes on to add, 'Yet another typical mistake many people make is trying to get everything right away. If you have set many goals that are in no way connected to each other, then the whole of your mental energy will be in vain, dispersed into emptiness.'[5]

The message, time and time again, from different sources, is that we need to focus, and persevere with our focus. But how do we develop these abilities?

Ingredients for perseverance

The ingredients for perseverance are:

> allowing uninterrupted *focus* by removing internal distractions;

> cultivating *self-discipline* and dedication to the object of your focus.

These two are intertwined. Self-discipline is a character strength that helps you dedicate yourself to a goal; in order to dedicate yourself to a goal, you also have to be able to focus your attention like a laser on that goal (and 'focus away' from all sorts of other distractions clamouring for your attention).

---

5. Vadim Zeland – *Reality Transurfing Vol. 2.*

Focus and internal distractions

Even when most people already have a clear enough goal in mind – they already have a point B to set their sights on – they may not succeed in getting to point B if they do not have the necessary endurance to deal with other distractions along the way and stick to the path when success is not certain (dealing with uncertainty).

Most people could take steps to improve their lives (income, job prospects, health, social circles) considerably. They could research and apply for better jobs, train to update their skills, start a small business on the side, write a book that is waiting to be written, raise their level of activity and physical fitness, or network more for professional or personal gain. But most people do not do these things, even when it's in their obvious interest to do so.

Instead, most people will procrastinate – which is a fancy word for saying they will avoid, put off or allow themselves to be distracted by unrelated things.

What are some of the distractions that tempt people off their chosen path and derail their sense of focus and application? Most people would name the usual suspects: Facebook, video games, books, something to eat or drink, being 'preoccupied' by worrying about other things, accepting offers of distractions from friends, a sudden urge to do other, irrelevant work.

I would like you to consider that even though having to check your email yet again requires an external, physical aspect (your computer hardware), for me that does not qualify as a true external distraction. An external distraction is when the building has to be evacuated due to a fire drill, or a power cut prevents you from using your computer, or your country is annexed by an invader, forcing you to abandon your business. These are truly external things that are out of your control.

'Having' to check your Facebook updates is merely a reflection of your internally distracted state, and constitutes an internal distraction.

Your main source of distraction therefore arises from an internal battlefield. The external environment is merely a mirror reflecting what you manage to overcome inside.

If our internal environment is a battlefield, then who are we fighting? Our two key internal opponents are *pain* and *pleasure*. It is a lifelong struggle to tame these two and put them in their place. They often forget that they are just your 'special advisers', while you are the 'president' of your mind and body.

Meet pain and pleasure

Our nervous system is designed to pursue pleasure and avoid pain. This simple rule of thumb has served us well in our evolution.

Life was a lot simpler and basic back in prehistoric times. There were things that threatened our survival because they wanted to eat or kill us (so we needed to avoid or fight them), and there were those things we needed to pursue to continue our survival (food, mates, social alliances).

We had our hands full taming nature until relatively recently. In the last few hundred years (a tiny glitch in evolutionary terms), we have largely conquered nature, at least in the developed world – we have killed off or can fend off all our predators; we have mass housing and mass food production; and there are laws, regulations and police forces to protect us. Most of us no longer experience daily life-or-death challenges to our survival. However, we still have two very dedicated bodyguards left over as remnants from those times – Pain and Pleasure still insist on advising you on your decisions *as if your survival were at stake*. They think they know best, but they are out of touch with the vastly changing times.

Like it or not, these two are going to be with you for the rest of your life. You might as well get to know them and learn how to handle them, so that you make the best of the situation.

Pain

Mr Pain is very 'pain averse'. His knee-jerk reaction is to shy away from anything that could cause pain – not just potential physical pain, but also *emotional* or *psychological* pain, such as stress, tension, anxiety and uncertainty.

Mr Pain is therefore the chief reason why you feel an instinctive reluctance at the prospect of applying effort, exertion and dedication in pursuit of something that is not a guaranteed success. Pain wants to spare you from experiencing the stress of the hard work involved, the anxiety caused by uncertainty, and the pain from any wasted effort or disappointment, or any potential conflict that could hurt you.

As such, it's in Pain's nature to be:

> Looking for the path of least resistance. In ancient times, it would have been best to conserve energy just in case available food stocks were low, or in case our life was suddenly on the line and we needed to leap into action.

> Risk-averse. He's a great fan of safety and certainty (i.e. comfort zones).

> Focusing mostly on avoiding any immediate or short-term pain. He is not great at thinking strategically or in terms of the bigger picture. For instance he will put off a small pain in the present (avoiding an injection, or a trip to the dentist, going to the gym, etc) without considering that this might cause a larger pain for his 'boss' in the future. As far as he is concerned, that's the job of future Mr Pain, not current Mr Pain. That's someone else's shift!

Pleasure

Ms Pleasure seeks to escape from pain (e.g. stress or tension) by having lots of lovely distractions. She loves indulging in the pleasures available in the moment. She prefers immediate gratification or a small pleasure in the now to being self-disciplined and patient in order to get a bigger pleasure in the future. Like Mr Pain, she doesn't give much thought to the future.

She shies away from boredom, tedium or exertion and doesn't believe that these qualities could be beneficial or wise. She wants to enjoy life and max out on the nice stuff while minimising the other stuff.

Both Mr Pain and Ms Pleasure act like teenagers. They want to sit at home watching TV and playing video games, or having long baths and massages all day.

Your role

You are the leader, the president, the decision-maker – not pain, and not pleasure. They, your advisers, should just advise, rather than taking over the decision-making directly.

Do not abdicate leadership to your subordinates. They work for you, not the other way around. They don't know how to do your managerial job and they will make a mess of things if put in charge. They will drain the treasury or press the nuclear button when spooked by the sabre-rattling posturing of another country.

Your advisers expect you to overrule them if you feel strongly enough about a different policy. If you do not assert your difference of opinion, then they will assume their case is stronger than yours and that you agree with them.

Remember that your advisers are employed *only* to look out for you and offer advice about the world in certain limited perspectives. Pain will only look out for the potential *pain* in things. Pleasure will only look out for the *pleasurable distraction* options.

When people only have one way of looking at the world, they will respond to events in very limited 'frames' or ways. As a famous psychotherapist once commented, 'If all you have is a hammer, everything begins to look like a nail.' These partial advisers will only end up giving you a very distorted view of reality. The problem is that they forget they can only see the world in this way and that there is always more to the picture.

You, on the other hand, possess an objectivity that they lack. It is your job to consult with them and acknowledge their advice, but to steer the 'government' towards the best path for the greater good. You will often need to be patient, educating them about the bigger picture and the better long-term strategies and rewards available.

If we only ever listened to Pain or Pleasure, then nothing worthwhile would get done. For instance, I expect that on many occasions in your life, you embarked on a project that ended up being more hard work than you imagined at the beginning. It could have been studying for a qualification, joining a team, renovating a house, starting an apprenticeship or having a baby. It's likely that if, at the beginning, you had a crystal ball that would give you a glimpse of the work involved, Mr Pain would go into overdrive, screaming: 'What the hell do you think you're getting into? There's no way we can deal with that kind of stress/demand/challenge. Get away from here as fast as you can!' The doubt would have set in and you would have declined the challenge.

So it's just as well that Pain doesn't have access to a crystal ball, because he would have led you to miss out on some amazing experiences, achievements and growth opportunities.

Confidence is a good quality to have. The more confident we are, the more 'risks' we take, the more achievements and success we end up having, and the more we will have packed our lives with enriching, fulfilling experiences. How do we gain such a desirable quality as confidence?

Confidence is a muscle, which grows in response to healthy stimulation (exposure to challenges). The more you allow yourself to be challenged, the stronger your muscle becomes.[6] Confidence allows

---

6. Just like a real muscle, the key is 'healthy stimulation'. Over-stimulating a muscle in the gym will lead to damage or burn out. Keep a healthy balance in mind.

you to keep expanding your comfort zones, to add more and more previously challenging demands to the repertoire of things you can now handle. If you don't exercise this muscle enough, then you will never know your full potential.

I'm a fan of the TV programme *MasterChef*. The sheer hard work that the applicants go through is astounding and seems hellish to someone who doesn't love cooking. Applicants need to sustain focused attention for hours, multi-tasking to cook several different things at once, or prepare hundreds of plates of food. By the end of the challenges, the applicants are spent and drained, but they are also elated about their achievements. They have asked more of themselves than they ever before, dug deep and delivered, and achieved more than they had ever imagined they would. Consequently their confidence and expertise as chefs takes a quantum leap, which they are obviously delighted and proud about.

By the way, another thing I have noticed about the most successful applicants goes back to a point I made in Chapter 1 – all of them have a passion for being the best chef they can possibly be. They want to know their fullest potential and are pursing a larger value in the context of cooking.

This sense of elation and leap in confidence is something I myself have observed many times, particularly in the different people I worked with in two BBC TV series about extreme phobias. The show arranged very daunting challenges for its subjects, ranging from skydiving to stand-up comedy. The participants started off doubting their ability to cope with the challenge, but at the end felt ecstatic to have done so, and put into perspective their previously held beliefs about their abilities to deal with their phobias.

In the absence of testing ourselves, we remain in our default state, which is a tendency to underestimate our selves and our levels of resilience. At the outset we tend to doubt our ability to pull through tough times and challenges. In this state, Mr Pain's beliefs remain untested and unchallenged, and you keep your confidence levels artificially low.

Some more will be said on dealing with pain in the next two chapters. For now, be prepared for Mr Pain's tendency to over-react to new challenges in certain predictable and limited ways. Don't fall for his hype. It is your job to remember this, as president of the overall wellbeing of your mind and body, whenever you are listening to Mr Pains' advice.

As for Ms Pleasure, you can also think of her as trying to make you escape from pain by retreating into creature comforts. This is where self-discipline comes in.

Self-discipline

Self-discipline is the ability to motivate oneself despite distractions, temptations or feeling tired or low. In this section, I'll be focusing on dealing with the temptations part, and later I will deal with self-discipline in terms of sustaining motivation despite feeling negative.

Staying focused on a desirable and healthy goal, and ignoring temptations and distractions, requires a very important quality – *delaying immediate gratification*. Remember, by nature we are programmed to take the path of least resistance (the easy path to conserve energy) and to indulge our appetites when there is the opportunity to do so. For our ancestors, when a glut of food was available, it made sense to gorge on that surplus food, because famine might be lurking round the corner.

The idea of delaying an available pleasure in the moment in order to reap a bigger or better pleasure in the future is likely a relatively novel concept in our evolution. Nevertheless, it's how the modern world works. Let's face it, on any given day there are an enormous number of distractions that can derail our momentum, available at our fingertips. We can order anything online, for example, and often it can be delivered right away for our convenience. Self-discipline is the ability to disregard all these fleeting pleasures in dogged pursuit of a worthy goal that will make you and others much happier down the line.

Poor discipline simply means inconsistent action. You make a good start, but then you do not keep at it long enough to achieve your worthwhile goal.

When you are working toward a goal, you have to look out for sneaky or covert distractions – activities that Ms Pleasure or Mr Pain will convince you are relevant to your goal, but are actually just red herrings and smoke screens they throw in your path to 'rescue' you from your hard work and effort.

The major covert distraction is 'majoring in minors' – the sudden urge to re-organise your CD collection alphabetically, or weed out useless emails from your inbox folder, or repaint your room, or whatever. Of this group of 'majoring in minors', the most insidious distraction itself is excess planning. I remember a student at university who found a great pretext to avoid knuckling down and actually revising the content for the exams. He would spend hours making elaborate folders about *how* he was going to study, complete with colour-coded paper notes and dividers. His folders were beautiful. He kept running out of time when it came to the actual studying part, but didn't feel too bad, because he justified to himself that at least he had been 'working'. Obviously too much energy put into planning means there is less available for implementation.

How to delay immediate gratification

There are a number of ways for delaying immediate gratification:

a) Name the game.

b) See the bigger picture.

c) Ramp up your worthwhile goal.

Name the game

This is a variation on how you learnt to deal with Pain in the earlier part of this chapter. It is about understanding that Pleasure or Pain will invariably interpret your options in certain prejudiced and limited ways, and will then lobby you in the hope of derailing you off any longer, harder (but more rewarding) path, back onto the shorter, easier path of least resistance and immediate gratification.

Knowing their game means you can call them out in it. You can choose to have no part of their game and thus not be drawn into their model of the world.

See the bigger picture

Seeing the bigger picture means considering the process in terms of what I refer to as 'a time to reap and a time to sow'. When you can see the larger process involved in the pursuit of a desirable goal, you recognise that, prior to the lovely reward (the reaping phase), there is an earlier, necessary phase of investment, which constitutes the price for your goal (the sowing phase). You can't reap unless you sow first.

In 2012, London hosted the Olympic Games. The UK did very well in the medals table and UK athletes inspired many people throughout the country. We viewers saw fit young people turning up for a race, running, swimming and jumping with God-like strength, speed, skill and grace, and winning medals – all to the adulation of an adoring home crowd, with fame and sponsorship deals thrown in.

What we were seeing was those athletes enjoying the *reaping* phase. Who wouldn't want to win a gold medal for their country in front of huge audience? What we didn't see nearly so much of was the far longer *sowing* phase, the endless, often solitary, repetitive practice behind the scenes. Elite athletes recognise the sowing phase and are mentally prepared to pay the price in the hopes of reaping, for example, that coveted gold medal.

The lesson I take from this is that if I embark on a desirable goal (e.g. writing this book!), there comes a time when there is nothing for it but to knuckle down, put pen to paper, get writing and keep writing for a certain amount of time every day. There is no way around that. However, making the necessary sacrifices – turning down pleasurable alternatives to write instead – is easier to do if I say to myself, 'OK, here comes the sowing phase'. In this way, I take responsibility for owning the price of my goal and getting through it. Because I have mentally accepted the need for the sowing phase as a necessary stepping-stone to my goal, I am psychologically prepared for it.

So when you consider a desirable goal, gear up for the unavoidable investment or sowing phase. That will focus your intent and concentration and help you to ignore distractions and temptations.

Remember: the quicker you get on and sow, the sooner you can reap the rewards and put sowing behind you.

Ramp up your goal

To achieve your goal, the temptation of experiencing a pleasurable distraction needs to be replaced by the even bigger pleasure you will receive from pursuing your goal.

For example, I've always had a soft spot for chocolate muffins. In my twenties, I had a higher metabolism, did a lot more exercise and could pretty much eat what I wanted without it coming back to bite me. I got used to eating chocolate muffins on any whim or fancy that took me, without seeming to pay a price.

Fast forward twenty years into the future and that is no longer the case. Now being slim and healthy is not a given, but something that requires conscious application. When I go to the supermarket and walk down the bread aisle, I always see the row of muffins nearby tempting me. Whenever I see them Pleasure says, 'Ooh, double choc-chip, that would taste great. We could just reach over and put some in the trolley.'

Now, instead of reaching out automatically, my 'president' or conscious mind responds with: 'You know, I'm not going to lie to you. They would taste great and there would be pleasure for about, what, 40–50 seconds? But I want to remind you that I also feel a lot of pleasure seeing myself on a different path where I remain slim, fit and healthy, feeling really good and proud of my body. So which is it to be? A path where I have a small, fleeting pleasure that is quickly over once I have to wear this muffin somewhere on my stomach, or a path where you see me slim, fit and happier in the long term?'

Ms Pleasure replies, 'Oh well, when you put it that way, I suppose I prefer your chosen course of action, because there are a lot more things in it to feel pleasure about.' Result: the right path has clearly dominated in pleasure terms when weighed up against the alternative path of eating a muffin. One little muffin weighed against being slimmer, healthier, more confident, more proud and feeling virtuous is just no contest. I get to walk away from the muffin selection feeling pretty pleased with myself, and seconds later forget all about it – and it didn't even take any effort! This was not done through willpower, but by working on my values.

> Whenever you are faced with such a temptation, acknowledge to yourself that if you take the easy path, you will feel a small, fleeting pleasure (whether it is for sweets, food, video games, gambling).

> Consider an alternative option for a greater pleasure, which really ramps up and overtakes the pleasure that could be gained from the alternative scenario.

> Present this choice to Ms Pleasure, with a beefed-up, bigger, more desirable long-term value pitted against a small, insignificant, minor, fleeting value in the present.

Armed with these approaches you will have everything you need to start wrestling with Pain and Pleasure and win! Being able to tame these two will give your powers of focus and perseverance a massive boost.

The power of momentum

I have found that any long-term endeavour, whether it's going to the gym, writing a report or doing the huge laundry pile, requires us to face a universal obstacle: overcoming inertia.

Inertia is the resistance of any physical object to a change in its state of motion or rest. Applied to the field of psychology, I take this to mean that any initial change in the status quo will be painful, so avoidance is the first knee-jerk reaction.

The first step requires the most effort and energy, and that's why most people stumble at the very first hurdle. When you come up against initial resistance, your system is protesting that you have kicked it out of its usual comfort zone; it's hoping to avoid whatever pain, such as boredom, the task might involve. It's like having to get out of your nice cosy bed on a winter's day.

Moreover, your system mistakenly believes that this surge in pain, experienced at the first hurdle, will remain constant, i.e. that you will just go on facing more of the same. This self-sabotaging belief saps your resolve. I mean, who'd want to face a seemingly endless, hopeless uphill struggle?

Here's where a reality check is needed. Once the initial inertia is overcome, most tasks actually get a whole lot easier. Just like pushing a car up a bit of an incline, as the incline changes into a decline, all you need to do is pop back in and let the downhill momentum carry you forward. With a little bit of perseverance, you give yourself the chance to see that your efforts will be rewarded, that you don't have to keep expending the same amount of energy as you did at the beginning, and that it won't be as painful later as it was at the start.

It's all about momentum. A passenger plane expends more energy getting airborne than it will need for the rest of most of its trips. After it's up in the sky, and can take advantage of assistance from thermals and coast. A bit later, the pilot can fly the plane on auto-pilot.

In order to 'get on a roll' with momentum, you need action. A little daily or frequent action towards a goal begins to move it, like nudging a big boulder that is perched on a cliff.

The wonderful thing about momentum is that if you do take frequent action towards a goal, you don't have to keep going through the same motivation process each time. For example, once I started going to the gym and gained some momentum, I didn't have to force myself to go every subsequent time. I was on a roll.

Once I gained momentum in writing my book, it became far easier to sit down each day, turn on my computer and then keep clarifying and elaborating my thoughts. I went on my own kind of auto-pilot mode.

So, in short – if you want momentum help you to your goals, you need to give yourself the chance to build some momentum in the first place, by overcoming initial inertia. After that, it's often plain sailing.

In summary

> Perseverance represents steady persistence in a course of action, a purpose or a particular state, especially in spite of difficulties or discouragement.

> Many successful people in their field became successful because they were *clear* about what they wanted and then *persevered* in getting what they wanted.

> To enable you to persevere, you need to allow uninterrupted *focus* by removing internal distractions and cultivating *self-discipline* and dedication to the object of your focus.

> Our own internal environment is a battlefield that undermines our

dedication, commitment and focus to our goals.

> Our two main internal sources of conflict are pain and pleasure.

> Your role is to put them in their place by realising they are only special advisers to your President role. They are not meant to take over your job and make all the decisions.

> Pain has a tendency to overreact to new challenges in certain predictable and limited ways. Don't fall for his hype.

> You can tame Pleasure by cultivating self-discipline. Self-discipline is the ability to motivate oneself despite distractions.

> Some ways to increase self-discipline include:
  - Naming the game.
  - Seeing the bigger picture and understanding when there is a time to reap and a time to sow.
  - Ramping up your worthwhile goal so that it dominates all other unworthy goals.

> Inertia can be overcome by building unstoppable momentum, which in turn comes from taking consistent, frequent action in pursuit of a goal until momentum is built.

CHAPTER EXERCISE – THE CHOICE 2

Sorry, but I'm going to have to use the Choice of Two Paths format again. It's just such a wonderful, all-round, powerful technique for clarification of values and motivation. So here goes:

> Imagine a choice of paths awaits you. A path to the left and a path to the right.

> The path to the left represents you indulging in some very short-term gratification – any distraction, such as food, using the internet, or making social phone calls.

> The path to the right is longer but offers a far bigger reward down the line.

> Turn and face the left path and imagine you could time-travel down this virtual future until the point immediately after you have engaged in your immediate gratification.

> Be aware that now is the time to 'pick up the tab' for that gratification – excess calories you didn't want; wasting time you wanted to spend elsewhere; missed opportunities, whether personal or professional. Let the true cost of picking up the tab for this behaviour sink in here.

> Now rewind and go back to the beginning of the fork in the road and turn towards the path to the right. Start travelling down the path to the right, this time remaining steadfast and dedicated to your goal. You see yourself accepting and working through the necessary sowing phase, all the while feeling you are getting closer and closer to the great rewards at the end. Finally, you reach the time to reap, and here you amp up all the benefits. Feel everything about the greater pleasure experienced at this end point. Let that really soak into your awareness.

> Now rewind back to the beginning. A choice of paths awaits you and by now you should be able to look at your choices in a different light. You have begun to associate pain with the path to the left, and

pleasure with the path to the right. You know that if you stray from the right path, you will miss out on all the pleasures awaiting you at the end. You know that you cannot have the benefits of the path to the right with the behaviour of the path to the left. Something has to give. Change means you are willing to do whatever is needed to have the life of the right path.

> Make a choice and, when you do, accept responsibility for doing whatever the 'price of that path' requires of you.

CHAPTER 4: BEING IRREVERENT IN THE FACE OF OBSTACLES

I am always doing things I can't do. That's how I get to do them.

– Pablo Picasso

I really admire the above comment by Picasso. I imagine all the people who were trying to project their limited beliefs onto him about what he could or couldn't do, and Picasso just brushing these limitations aside with irreverence while he found the limits of his potential for himself.

Becoming irreverent[7] in the face of obstacles makes perseverance a lot easier, because it makes light of the challenges in your path and thus minimises their powers to scare you off or block you.

I have found the following tried-and-tested tips to be very useful in increasing my irreverence when I'm up against obstacles, helping me to laugh more in the face of fear and tweak the nose of Pain.

They are:

1. Am I driven by beliefs or reality?
2. So what?
3. Reducing importance
4. Mountains into molehills
5. Stay with it

---

7. The book *Irreverence* by Cecchin, Lane and Ray (1992, Karnac Books) is the inspiration behind my use of this term. The authors suggest we cultivate a healthy 'irreverence' about beliefs. I have adopted this notion with the intent of applying it towards general obstacles in our way.

1. Am I driven by beliefs or reality?

Our brains have a tendency to opt for a lazy auto-pilot mode (conserving that precious energy again) rather than a curious scientist mode.

Whenever we go into auto-pilot mode, we are driven by our pre-existing beliefs and expectations, rather than what is actually happening out there in reality. A true scientist, on the other hand, draws her conclusions after reviewing all available evidence, not before she's even studied anything.

In auto-pilot mode, we lazily fall back on stereotypes, rules of thumb passed down from others around us, which save us the effort of having to come up with new theories from scratch. Some of these stereotypes and biases are well known in psychology. We have stereotypes about other cultures and nationalities, about gender, race, religion, sports, politics, and so on.

But we also have stereotypes about ourselves. We often fall back on beliefs about ourselves that are well out of date and not in touch with present reality. We may still believe we need to eat the same amount of food we did when we were ravenous 20-year-olds; we may still believe we need the nine hours sleep we needed when we were teenagers, when in fact we seem to be fine with fewer hours; we may still believe we are small, vulnerable, five-foot-nothing eight-year-olds at the mercy of older and taller children, instead of the strapping grown men or women we are now.

In short, our brains are a bit like a computer that needs constant software upgrades to deal with all the new developments happening around us. We humans regularly fail to carry out updates by testing our beliefs against new developments, because frankly it's just too much work when it is easier to go into auto-pilot. We usually need a bit of an incentive or kick up the backside to override the auto-pilot mode and go more scientist-mode to check our beliefs against reality.

Some people, of course, will fail to do this because they get attached to their beliefs and have problems with their judgement being questioned. In which case, they prefer to spend more energy defending their beliefs than it would take to upgrade them. But I digress.

The point I am coming to is that, all too often, our beliefs are not harmless hypotheses hanging around until further clarification about them is gained. Once we believe something, our bodies react as if that belief might as well be true. Just ask someone who is terrified of spiders to imagine a spider, and he or she will shiver in fear even when they know they are in a completely secure room.

So when we have pre-existing beliefs about success – the effort it will require, doubt about our abilities, not knowing how to go about starting the process – our bodies will not remain passively on standby. Instead they launch an active distress response, doing their best to help us avoid feared scenarios that don't even exist in reality! And the conscious mind – the President or decision-maker – will often collude with the body and buy into this whole artificial reality, rather than taking a moment to point out that it's not real.

There are countless psychological experiments showing how easily our brains can be duped and deceived. One simple experiment that comes to mind is asking someone to decide whether a blue room or an identical red room is warmer. Most people answer that they feel warmer in the red room, when in fact both rooms are at identical temperatures. The brain has a nice little pre-existing stereotype about colour to fall back on when making a decision like this, which says, 'blue things are cold and red things are warm'.

There are also many magicians and illusionists on TV who frequently demonstrate how easily we are influenced by subtle cues such as music, lighting, clothes and mannerisms to manipulate our decisions. In fact, I recently watched a programme on the National Geographic channel called *Test Your Brain*. In this programme, a magician was drawing the viewer's attention to his hands while people dressed variously as rabbits, bears and gorillas went unnoticed in the background, despite these actors being very obviously present when the clip was rewound. Not to mention the countless experiments demonstrating the placebo effect, with patients overcoming crippling worry, allergies, physical pain and smoking simply by taking pills that they believed would help them, but were in fact just sugar pills.

The case is irefutable: the parts of our brains running our sensory perceptions cannot be trusted.

In that case, I refuse to take seriously any part of my brain that is trying to convince me I am in grave danger when I'm thinking about attending a party (because it is convinced everyone is looking at me and judging me) or that a dog sitting calmly by its owner must want to bite my hand off, or that I shouldn't apply for a job in case I don't get it (which it seems to think is something I could never recover from!). I have grown used to dismissing my out-of-proportion sensory feedback, preferring to test out my senses' theories for myself, rather than just believing them offhand.

Knowing what Pain and the whole sensory feedback department are like, I tend to question their credibility when they bring flawed case after flawed case to my attention, claiming that the whole world is out to harm me. Imagine if you grew up alone on a desert island, then got rescued and integrated with mainstream society. At one point you remark how the sky looks extra clear and 'green' today. The people around you look at each other, shake their heads sadly, and inform you that you are mistaken, because the sky is blue not green. In fact, they inform you that you can go out and ask the same question to as many other random people as you wish, and they will nearly all say the same thing.

What would you do? Your visual senses are convinced that the sky is green. It seems so obviously, vividly and undeniably green. Do you choose to believe this contradictory information that the sky is blue, or do you dismiss it because it seems to be unbelievable based on your personal experience, and assume everyone else must be colour blind while you see true colours?

Knowing how easily duped my senses can be, I would be happy to take on board the notion that the sky, as strange as it seems to me, may actually be a different colour than the one I am perceiving. I have become aware of my sensory fallibility. A useful tip is to consciously go into scientist mode and ask, 'Am I being driven by beliefs or reality?' Adopting this mantra will get you used to becoming irreverent in the face of the obstacles brought about by your own sensory feedback.

2. So what?

The 'So what?' attitude is another useful way to test your senses' inflated ideas about what might pose a potential danger to your welfare. For instance, suppose you wanted to apply for a career that was different from the kind of career your neighbours would expect you to go into. Mr Pain will confidently try and tell you this will result in something catastrophic, such as other people not approving of your job choice. Pain tends to think this rationale is sufficient justification for doing things his way.

If you were to respond, however, with, 'OK, so some people may look down on my choice of job, so what?' Then Pain will be taken aback and shocked that his pronouncement did not have the desired effect. He's a bit like a doctor who is not used to being questioned by their patient.

Pain will retort with something like, 'Did you hear me correctly?

There is a clear and present danger that other people will disapprove of your job choice.'

You: Yes I heard, and I repeat, *so what*?

This is where Pain starts to flounder because he is not used to having to justify himself further than that.

Pain: Well, for a start … it won't feel nice.

You: OK, and if it doesn't feel nice, it doesn't feel nice. So what?

Pain: Well, uh, it might cause unbearable pain for you.

You: If they don't like my new job, that's their choice. I can't help the way other people feel, can I? If they really did care about me, they would support me, wouldn't they? So why would the opinion of some people who don't actually care about cause me 'unbearable pain'?

Pain: Uh, well, OK, it probably won't happen, but [*weakly*]… er, it could happen, couldn't it?

Get in the habit of no longer taking catastrophic outcomes as guaranteed. Question the basis of such conclusions from both your external and 'internal' advisers.

3. Reducing importance

Getting in the habit of irreverently saying 'So what?' in the face of unscientific feedback will deflate the importance you may historically have attached to these events and experiences.

If we attach too much importance to things, it ends up generating unnecessary pressure – for instance, in public speaking, going for a job interview or asking someone out on a date. When there is too much pressure, you end up creating a type of performance anxiety for yourself, which can end up paralysing you into inaction.

If you have an active, imaginative and creative brain, and you ask it to run potential disaster scenarios (in order to prepare you for them), your brain will endlessly try and attach importance to most of your outcomes in order to get your attention and make you take the 'threat' seriously. Your brain will say, 'You've got to nail this job interview, because if you don't get this job you might not get any other job, and if you don't get any job you will be penniless and no man/woman will have you, then your dream of kids will be gone and you will ultimately die alone and be forgotten … you MUST get this job or everyone around you will be disappointed and you will die alone, despised by all.'

So not much pressure then.

We need to rebalance things by continually reality-checking the level of importance we assign to things. In his book *Reality Transurfing* (vol 2), author Vadim Zeland gives a clear illustration of the way we attach excessive importance to how our appearance will be received by others. He writes: 'Physical appearance can only be judged by potential partners. That is a very small percentage of the population. Others could not care less about your appearance. You don't believe me? Then ask the most respected judge – yourself: how much do you care about the appearance of other people that are not part of the potential partner pool? Most likely, you have never thought about whether a given person is attractive or not. People around you are thinking the same (or not thinking at all) about you.

'You can be certain that this is the case, even if you consider yourself ugly. Ugliness makes an impression only when you meet someone for the first time. After that, ugliness is no longer noticed (once they have become accustomed to it).'

This is a great way of emphasising that we worry far more about the effect we might have on people than we really should.

If we attach too much importance to our appearance then we will perceive everything in those terms, for instance: 'You perceive everything that emanates from other people – looks, gestures, facial expressions, words – through your filter. What will you see? A friendly smile will turn into a grin. Someone's happy laughter will transform into gloating amusement at your expense. Two people are whispering to one another – they are gossiping about you. Someone briefly glanced at you – he or she gave you an angry look. Someone winced because their stomach hurt – oh God, what did he think of you? And finally, any compliment will turn into mockery. Yet, no one was actually thinking any of these thoughts. It is only in your head – it is your own [filter].'

The solution again: Zeland suggests we keep lowering the importance we automatically presume is attached to things and events around us. Things are rarely as important as we tend to think they are. In fact, it helps to intend to achieve the goal while also accepting the possibility of your defeat in advance. Plan for what you will do if you fail to achieve your goal.

The case of Lawrence: Accepting defeat in advance

Lawrence is a successful manager in his forties, married to Diane. They have three children ranging from five to nine years old. Lawrence and Diane have been having serious, ongoing relationship problems for many years that appear insurmountable, and came to me for counselling.

Lawrence was extremely anxious and agitated because he only wanted to consider one path – keeping the family together. His solution was to keep pushing Diane into therapy and reconciliation. It didn't help that his frustration levels were increasing and he became more demanding and irritable towards Diane, who subsequently found herself less inclined to consider reconciling with him.

Finally Lawrence came in one day looking far more peaceful. He informed me that he had accepted that divorce was a real possibility. He realised that there were pros and cons to both options of staying together or divorcing, and that he could also find happiness in alternative outcomes – that life didn't end just there.

Ironically, as soon as he accepted this possibility he was calmer and less pushy, and Diane felt more inclined to build bridges with him. They started getting on better than they had in a very long time.

Considering the 'defeat' scenario allows you to open up to other ways of achieving your ultimate goal that you hadn't considered. It doesn't lock you into just one 'do-or-die' mindset.

A proviso: I am not saying go over the defeat scenario again and again. Just fully consider it once, properly, enough to remove the pressure of the 'only one outcome' policy.

4. Mountains into molehills

Whenever we come up against some new challenge, you can be assured that Mr. Pain is going to be melodramatic, make a meal out of the situation, and try and talk you out of it. He will try to tell you, 'Oh boy, you are up against a mountain of effort and work that will be beyond your powers of endurance, so please try and look for an easier path.' He will try to make a mountain out of a molehill.

Needless to say, your job is to not buy into this hysteria and convert the mountain back into a molehill.

For the sake or argument, supposing I am given a thousand-piece jigsaw puzzle for Christmas (a lame present to receive at my age, I know, but bear with me). As I spill out the thousand pieces on the carpet in front of me, Pain has a fit: 'Oh my God, the pieces seem endless, there are too many things to do, this will be too difficult, no way can we do this', etc, etc. The conversation that follows goes something like this:

Calmly, Me: OK, I'm just going to do ten pieces today. Surely even you will agree that we can do ten pieces, right?

Pain: Yes, ten pieces is OK, but look at all the other …

Me: [*cutting him off*] We're just going to do ten today, OK? That's all, relax.

Me: [*a few minutes later*] OK, so we've done ten pieces and that wasn't hard was it? So tomorrow we can do another ten pieces, and then the day after another ten pieces, and each day will be equally easy.

Pain: Well, of course, yes, ten pieces is easy. That's not what I'm worried about.

Me: Whether we do ten pieces a day for ten days, or ten pieces a day for 20, 30 or even 100 days is actually unimportant. It's the same easy amount of work every day that we have nothing to fear from, right? Let's just keep doing the same amount of work until there is no more work left to do.

There is a similar analogy I've come across that makes the same point: if you had to eat a two-pound piece of salami, you would choke trying to eat it all in one go. But if sliced it into very thin pieces, you could calmly and steadily work your way through it and eventually eat the whole lot.

5. Stay with it

An extension on the idea of converting mountains back into molehills is the ability to *stay with* the initial distress caused by uncertainty and anxiety, so that you can move into the more constructive converting-into-molehills phase.

The first step in facing any challenge is always the most daunting. Uncertainty and doubt are at their peak – which of course means Mr Pain will be screaming at you to run for the hills. When we experience such an initial surge of anxiety, there is a strong instinct to panic and flee.

The advice is simple: just hang in there and stay with it. Give yourself a chance to build some momentum and see what can be done to convert these seeming obstacles down into molehills. You may be pleasantly surprised.

I expect in your life you have already proved yourself capable of this countless times. Think of all the instances in which you bought something that was complicated to set up, like a piece of technology for your TV that's accompanied by a huge remote control and manual, or a simple-looking piece of furniture that turns out to require assembly out of dozens and dozens of scary-looking parts. You could have repacked the whole thing and sent it back, but instead you stayed with the initial 'this looks too confusing stage' and began to work out little bits of the puzzle.

I suspect there are many potentially good authors out there with good stories to write, but they haven't written them because they remain stuck at the initial uncertainty phase. Their potential stories were not given the chance to take shape and form.

When I was first asked to write this book, I didn't know what I was going to write other than some basic ideas I thought would be relevant. These different ideas were jotted down one on top of the other, along with bits of content I had from other notes. It was a mishmash and looked like a mess. But as I stayed with it, I saw patterns and themes begin to emerge, becoming clearer and more coherent. Order was beginning to take shape out of chaos.

When faced with your challenge, stay with it through your initial uncertainty, knowing this is just the first part of a process and that things *will* become clearer as you continue. Give yourself time to build up some momentum and pretty soon you will see order emerging from the chaos in this new challenge too.

6. ACT

ACT simply stands for: *Action Cures Terror.*

ACT-ion is the antidote to 'paralysis by analysis'. Taking action requires courage. Courage is not the absence of fear, but acting *in spite* of the fear.

It will not by now come as a surprise to you that Mr Pain will feel nervous and undermined in the face of courageous intent and will try to regain some control. Mr Pain, you will recall, is risk-averse and wants you to stay in guaranteed safety (i.e. in your comfort zones). As you embark on any bold new move, he will say to you: 'Now look here … are we really going to do this thing? I mean that's not what we do, is it? Is that really us? Let's just stop and think about all the worst case scenarios here for a moment, shall we?'

Pain wants you to return to your 'normal' senses and usual, automatic programming. When he tries to do this, you need to ACT immediately to stop him hijacking your budding courage. Prevent him from trying to talk you into the *reasons* why you won't be able to get your results. Actions gets results – reasons for not acting don't. I've seen many patients talk themselves out of action and talk themselves back into a fear state.

In the Air Force, when a paratrooper goes on his first jump and some glitch happens to scare them, there is a policy of immediately getting the cadet back on the next parachute jump before their fear and doubt sets into permanent belief, and they start talking themselves out of any future jumps. The Air Force realise that they need to nip this analysis in the bud before it sprouts and takes root.

Again I am not asking you to always simply act and disregard the consequences of your choices. I am asking you to ACT when you *know* inside that your goal is desirable and achievable. I'm asking you to ACT when you have seen others already achieve the outcome before you, and it is now your turn; they are waiting and rooting for you, and all that stops you is feeling blocked or scared in some way.

To remind you to ACT, two sayings come to mind: *Do the thing you fear most and the death of fear is certain,*[8] and *Where there is no risk, there is no pride in anything you accomplish, so there can be no happiness.*[9]

---

8. Quote attributed to Mark Twain.
9. Quote attributed to Ted Nicholas.

7. Humour

Humour acts as a wonderful release agent for tension, and can make a difficult situation more bearable, so is another useful member of the irreverence team. It helps deflate the importance of a situation and makes it mundane instead. It can belittle anxiety and uncertainty and help you make light of a problem.

I am suggesting you look at your challenging situation and reframe it in a humorous way. I am not saying that, when faced with a challenge, you should turn to your nearest neighbour and say, 'Hey, listen, a rabbi, a priest and a vicar walk into a bar …' What I have in mind is a 'lite' version of gallows humour.

Gallows humour is humour that's applied in circumstances where death appears to be impending and unavoidable. For instance, there is a joke about a man who is about to be executed. The firing squad leader offers the man a cigarette and he replies, 'No thanks, I'm trying to quit.'

The military is full of gallows humor, as those in the services continually live with the danger of being killed. The original fathers of 'dry wit', at least in recorded military history, were the ancient Greek Spartans. In fact, 'laconic humour' – the kind of dry wit and one-liners that action heros like James Bond are famous for – is named for Laconia, the home of the Spartans.

One famous example comes from when King Leonidas led his 300 Spartans on a one-way suicide mission to stop the mighty Persian war machine (which numbered several hundred thousand soldiers against a puny allied Greek force of about 7,000). When the Spartan soldier Dienekes was told that the Persian archers were so numerous that, when they fired their volleys, their arrows would blot out the sun, he responded with, 'So much the better, we'll fight in the shade.'

On another occasion, Philip II of Macedon turned his attention to Sparta and sent a message: 'Surrender without further delay, for if I bring my army into your land, I will destroy your farms, slay your people, and raze your city.'

The Spartan leaders wrote back with a one-word reply: 'If.'

Next time someone tries to helpfully remind you of your limitations or inability to succeed in the face of a challenge, take a leaf out of Dienekes or James Bond's book, and say something irreverent (out loud or in your mind!). You will feel more like a warrior when you do.

You can also use humour in a slightly different way, to belittle the sources of worry. For instance, I tend to think of nagging Mr Pain as if he were my grandmother. She would fuss and fret over the most trivial concerns and try to advise me accordingly. It's very hard to take a military adviser seriously if he is dressed or sounds like your worried grandmother. This neatly flips the anxiety problem – instead of you being the one with the issue, he is the one who needs help.

8. Good news, bad news, who knows?

This phrase refers to a wonderful little Taoist parable I heard many decades ago that has helped me be more philosophical during times of adversity.

According to Taoism, the true significance of events can never be understood as they are occurring, for in every event there are elements of both good and bad. Furthermore, each event has no specific beginning or end, and may influence future events for years or even centuries to come.

This is illustrated in the following parable of the Taoist farmer. There was once a farmer whose only horse broke out of the corral and ran away. The farmer's neighbours, all hearing the news, came to the Taoist farmer's house to view the corral. They all said, 'Oh what bad luck! Your only horse has abandoned you. This is terrible news!' The Taoist farmer replied, 'Good news, bad news, who knows?'

About a week later, the horse returned, bringing with it a whole herd of wild horses, which the Taoist farmer and his son quickly corralled. The neighbours all came to see for themselves. 'Oh, what good luck!' they said. 'You have regained your horse, plus many new horses. You are rich. This is great news!'

The Taoist farmer replied, 'Good news, bad news, who knows?'

The next day, the farmer's only son tried to ride one of the new horses and was thrown off, breaking his leg. Again the neighbours returned to observe the situation, lamenting, 'Your only able-bodied son is now unable to work with you. You must be so upset. This is awful news.'

The Taoist farmer replied, 'Good news, bad news, who knows?'

At the same time, in China, a war was going on between two rival warlords. The warlord of the Taoist farmer's village was involved in this war. In need of more soldiers, he sent one of his captains to the village to conscript young men to fight in the war. When the captain came to take the Taoist farmer's son he found a young man with a broken leg, delirious with fever. Knowing there was no way the son could fight, the captain left him there. A few days later, the son's fever broke. The neighbours all came to see him. As they stood there, each one said, 'Oh what good luck!'

The Taoist farmer replied, 'The Taoist farmer replied, 'Good news, bad news, who knows?'

And so the story goes on indefinitely.

Back in 1996, I was working in Ireland as an area manager of some stores when I received a telephone call from London. My parents had been divorced for over 16 years and my mother hardly ever spoke to my father, so it was a big surprise to hear my father on the phone, saying he had been contacted by the porter of my mother's flat. My mother had left the door open, was lying in bed insisting she was about to die, and wanted a priest for last rites. My father suggested I get over to London right away, which I did.

I returned to quite a chaotic situation and had multiple points of urgency. My mum needed to be sent to my grandparents' home in Crete where they could look after her and she could at least have people around her all the time. Then I needed to sort out her flat (with the aim of selling it, as she could not cope on her own in London anymore). I had to organise meetings with a doctor, a solicitor (to get power of attorney) and estate agents, and book flights.

Then I had to empty my mother's flat (no easy feat given she had a moderate case of hoarding) in preparation for selling it. In between I also had to grieve about the realisation that the person I had got used to thinking of as my mother was no longer going to be that person.

By day, aside from dealing with multiple agents, I was also embroiled in haggling over the prices for items in the flat, which I needed to quickly sell at knockdown prices. By night, while my mother was still in the apartment before her flight to Crete, she would wake me up repeatedly throughout the night, claiming to see disturbing visions. I was only getting two to three hours sleep per night. I remember waking up seeing my pillow covered in hair, and passing blood in the toilet due to the physical and emotional stress.

Rather uncannily, like the parable of the Taoist farmer, I remember my neighbours lamenting my and my mother's fate, saying what dreadful news this was. And the parable of the farmer kept popping into my thoughts. I kept reminding myself, 'Good news, bad news, who knows?'

Once my mother had left and I took charge of the flat, I was advised by estate agents that the flat could sell for decent money, but not in the poor condition it was in. It needed to have the electrics rewired, the bathroom refitted, the seventies wallpaper removed, etc, etc. I decided to move back to London and spruce up the flat. I arranged to rent out some of the rooms while I worked on decorating and renovating each one in turn, funded by the rent from my new tenants, and fell into the role of landlord.

I had always wanted to retrain as a psychologist, but reasoned that I could never afford to do so. I could not afford to pay for the training, plus living costs. I simply did not have the means. Then it occurred to me that I now had a job as a landlord. I could work as a landlord in lieu of paying rent and get the rest on loans, which would not now be too prohibitive. I realised that for the first time, I had the viable means to pursue a new career.

I enrolled in a psychology course and entered into a vocation I have loved ever since. I've had the opportunity to help many other people overcome their own problems in turn, and the flat is managed as a beautiful private clinic.

As I look back on that time in 1996, as difficult as it was, a lot of good came about later as a result of it too – in fact, so many good things that it is doubtful whether they could ever have happened otherwise. In addition, this difficult period lent a quantum boost to my personal levels of resilience. I often think to myself 'If I can get through that intact, I can get through anything.'

Good news, bad news, indeed.

9. Make the best of any situation

The parable of the Taoist farmer will already help you make the best of any given situation, but there is another role model who can inspire us to make the best of any situation. That person is Epictetus.

Epictetus was a Roman slave of Greek origin, who was mistreated and abused by a harsh master. You think we've got it tough? Think about poor Epictetus, who did not have any rights as a slave and was beaten every day.

Epictetus took stock of his situation and, being of a philosophical disposition, grasped a very simple fact: when your ability to control external events is limited or nonexistent, you can learn to control your inner responses. He reasoned, 'Well, I haven't got any power or control over my situation or my master, so I have to accept that. The only area I have power in is my thoughts. I have power and control over what I let myself think. What I can do is commit myself on a daily basis to controlling my thoughts in a positive way to the best of my ability. I'm going to focus on questions and topics that interest me. I'm going to try to talk to other people who interest me. I'm going to try to control only what I can control, and leave the rest to forces that are beyond me.'

As Epictetus went about making the best of his situation, much to the surprise of his master, he became a really happy man – so much so that the master came to believe his slave was happier than even he was. So the master took Epictetus aside and asked him, 'What is your secret?'

Epictetus said, 'I simply believe in controlling my thoughts, and those parts of my life that I can control, and letting go of the rest. The more I do that, the happier I am.' His master was so impressed that he emancipated Epictetus and asked him to be his teacher. What a turn around of events for Epictetus, brought about by his resilience and positive thinking!

Remember the story of Epictetus and make the best of any difficult situation you find yourself in. It is hardly likely to be worse than his.

10. Character building

Throughout this chapter I've mentioned how it's useful to step back and consider the bigger picture – the underlying process at work, and the necessary stages involved in that process. For instance, suppose you would love to have a pony to ride on. You would do anything to keep that pony and suddenly the idea of mucking out stables doesn't seem so bad.

If you want to work for a powerful bank and start off by making the tea or working in the mailroom, you realise this is the time to pay your dues.

Trainee sumo wrestlers are given the task of wiping the bottoms of some of the larger professional wrestlers, who are so big they cannot reach to do it for themselves. The novice realises that this apprenticeship phase involves some less than desirable elements and that there is nothing for it but to grit his teeth and bear it if he wants to be a top wrestler in the future.

Trainee martial artists (or white belts) realise they will have to do lots of stretching and conditioning of their muscles if they want to kick as high and as gracefully as the black belts. They also know that until they gain the necessary skills, they are going to be at the mercy of the more experienced martial artists in any sparring contests. Again, white belts know that they need to suck it up and get on with it. That's how it goes. It's their time for sowing.

When you can see the constituent stages involved, it makes understanding and accepting them a lot easier. But it also offers one more realisation. It leads you to realise that you are embarking on a character-building process. People will voluntarily opt for a difficult path because they know it will be good for their development down the line – it will make a 'man' out of them, so to speak. I met quite a few people who got into martial arts because they were pain-averse and wanted to overcome their fears through exposure and desensitisation. They knew they were in for a few years of bruises and aches, but that it would do them good in the end.

Voluntarily undergoing necessary pain in order to build character is a healthy quality. It is the antidote to immediate gratification and helps build self-discipline.

So if you have just left college and want to get stuck in, working at the highest level among creatives, doctors, or black belts, but instead get offered the metaphorical 'tea boy' position instead, take a moment to consider the larger character-building process that is being offered to you.

Treat it like you are entering a martial arts dojo. A tough apprenticeship awaits you, but considering the longer term character-building process you are embarking on will help you sustain the resilience to see it through.

So there you have it – an extra toolkit of ten powerful tips for making you irreverent in the face of the obstacles in your chosen path. Apply them and you will increasingly see your challenges shrink and disappear.

In summary

> Becoming irreverent when faced with obstacles makes the job of perseverance a lot easier. The following tried-and-tested tips will help you develop this attitude.

- Ask yourself, 'Am I driven by beliefs or reality?'
- Say 'So what?' to the predictable panic from Mr Pain.
- Look to convert mountains into molehills.
- Make it through the initial phase of uncertainty in order to let your momentum build for the solution-focused parts.
- ACT – take action to immediately derail terror.
- In the face of a challenging situation, remind yourself: 'Good news, bad news, who knows?'
- Look to make the best of any situation, and it might turn out radically different than you expected.
- When faced with a long, daunting challenge, remember that you are embarking on a character-building process that will test you, but will pay off and be good for your development in the end.

CHAPTER EXERCISE – MOUNTAINS AND MOLEHILLS

The mountains-into-molehills approach is so effective for overcoming fears that it deserves to be looked at in more detail. Here are some methods by which you can break up any new challenge into manageable parts.

> Next time you are faced with a new or difficult-looking task, remember that your system has likely hyped it up into the mountain of obstacles that stands before you.

> Stay with the fear, knowing that your system has likely inflated the scale of the mountain, and that in any case, a mountain can be toppled and broken down into small, manageable molehills with enough time.

> In your mind's eye, see the mountain shrinking more and more into lots of easy-to-lift little boulders.

> Begin to reduce the mountain into smaller boulders – break down your problem (e.g. an essay or report, cleaning or decorating a room, learning a trade or a craft) into separate, discrete chunks.

> As you look at the 'boulders' surrounding you, start thinking about some kind of sequencing, as in: 'Well the first thing that would need to be done is this, followed by this, then that.'

> Once you have isolated the first two or three things to focus on, work on them until they are completed. That's your work for the day done.

> The next day, repeat the process, just like the analogy of the jigsaw I used earlier on. Complete a manageable day's work every day until you have run out of work to do.

> The next time you face a mountain, it is more likely you will say, 'It's OK, this looks like a hard mountain to overcome, but so did the last mountain, and by the end that seemed easy, so the same thing will apply here.'

As your wisdom and confidence build, you will increasingly find it easier to endure the 'stay with it' phase. Your resilience and perseverance will increase as you slowly but steadily tackle the mountain. Hey, you might even find yourself throwing in a quip or two in the face of adversity.

CHAPTER 5: TRUSTING IN SELF

Faith can move mountains. Doubt can create them.

– Howard Wight

Becoming irreverent when you are faced with obstacles is a lot easier when you develop solid trust in yourself – in your capabilities, determination and resilience.

When a large challenge presents itself to you, you will reduce the power of this new challenge to scare you if you remind yourself: 'While this challenge seems scary and looks like hard work, I have faith in myself and I believe I can pull this off.'

Try it and see how your new challenge feels in the face of this attitude.

You can also remind yourself that while you don't have all the answers up front, you just have to trust that, as a resourceful person, you WILL find the answers needed one way or another, as long as you commit to finding them.

And that, in a nutshell, is the difference between a confident and an unconfident person. Unconfident people are unconfident because they are anxious about future outcomes.

Scientifically speaking, on a spectrum ranging from 'much better than expected' to 'much worse than expected', outcomes could fall anywhere along on this continuum. So why do anxious, unconfident people invariably assume their outcomes will fall in the 'bad' to 'worse than expected' end of the spectrum?

The simple answer is that they do not *trust* the outcome to go well – or, to frame it inversely, *they trust that negative outcomes will happen.* They believe the outcome *must* turn out badly for them because they either do not trust others to behave nicely in the situation (e.g. others will laugh, ridicule or criticise them) or they do not trust 'life' (or God, or luck or fate) in general; or, even if others are well-meaning, anxious people may still feel insecure because they end up not trusting *themselves* to do what is needed to be done.

If unconfident people do actually achieve good results despite their prior negative expectations, they will tend to dismiss the impact of their own input in any positive process and instead attribute their success to luck (an impersonal factor outside of their control). That way they can safely default back to their old self-beliefs and not be troubled by contradictory evidence.

To reiterate – the common theme underlying the main difference between what makes a confident person or an unconfident person is always going to be that of *trust*. Simply put, the only difference between a confident person and an unconfident person is the *type* of trust they invest in.

If you were about to embark on a new endeavour – asking a person out on a date, going to see your favourite team play a key match, going for a job interview or meeting an important client – how worried would you still be if you had massive trust in others or yourself to do the best that can be done?

Even if you didn't get the date, that job or the new client, you would trust yourself to get results another time. You haven't given up. The war is not lost. You still feel hopeful of success.

The confident person mostly envisions a virtual reality in which they may have setbacks but they will ultimately achieve their goals. They assume it's just a matter of *when* they get good results, not *if*. Some of the favourite phrases of confident people are: 'It's just a numbers game' (a lucky hit over time is a given – i.e. demonstrates trust in *life*) and 'I'll think of something' (demonstrates trust in *self*).

The anxious person mostly envisions a virtual reality where the end goal is not being realised due to overwhelming obstacles. They are so stuck at the 'if' stage, that they can't consider the 'when'. Their favourite phrases are 'What if x happens' (where x equals any number of imaginative disasters and misfortunes) or 'I'm a realist.' Anxious people want risk-free guarantees or categorical certainty of success before committing to action.

There is an absolutely crucial, and normally overlooked factor, that is present in all your negative or positive virtual scenarios, and that is that whatever virtual scenario you envision will usually end up becoming *self-fulfilling*. Confident people who believe 'I'll think of something' invariably *do* think of something, or find assistance along the way, and end up with satisfactory outcomes. Anxious people generally perform worse, get unsatisfactory results and do not do themselves justice.

There does not have to be any magical law of attraction underlying these reasons. It's based on simple principles of cause and effect.

Imagine that you are single, and moreover, that you are fed up with being single. So you make a sincere promise to yourself that the next party you go to, you will ask someone out on a date, no matter who she or he is.

In due course you go to a party and see a stunning girl (or boy) standing there alone. Your heart drops because you believe this supermodel type is way out of your league. Still, you don't want to break your promise to yourself, so you will honour it and ask this perfect creature out.

How would you picture yourself doing this?

If, in your heart, you do not believe you stand a chance of success, would you approach your new love-idol in a self-assured way, or would you approach like a ball of quivering jelly, without a hope in hell, just wanting to get it over and done with so you can say 'I tried'?

And if you did the latter, how would you rate your chances of success?

If you believe there's little potential for a win, how much action will you be truly motivated to take? The answer is very little. It doesn't make any kind of sense to waste your energies on something you do not believe will make you a good return, whether it is dating, writing an essay or starting a business. Instead we would hold on to our precious energy and not commit to that course of action.

If you take very little action, what kind of results do you expect to get? The answer is simple – very little. And if you are getting very little results, then that's not doing anything to build *trust* in your abilities to get results in the future. In fact, the opposite is true. You will instead start trusting negative beliefs given by 'helpful' special advisers like Mr Pain, such as, 'It's time to get real and face it, you are not good at dating and should avoid it', or 'You have to accept that your lack of success might be because no one wants to be with you.'

Conversely, if you do believe something can be achieved, then you will be giving yourself a full green light to attack that goal without reservation. If you are throwing energy and action at an obstacle, the obstacle will become eroded and shrink under your onslaught. Once you have overcome your obstacle, your brain rewards you with a little dopamine hit, which leads to the kind of chest-thumping, whooping and general air-punching seen on any kind of TV reality show challenge or sports match. The dopamine hit makes you feel great, almost invincible, and it allows you to thumb your nose at Mr. Pain's earlier suggestion that your obstacle could not be overcome. 'Hah,' you say to yourself, 'next time I hear Pain's doom-mongering in the future, I'm just going to disregard it.' What you are in effect doing is withdrawing capital from your old investments in negative portfolios and investing them instead in positive portfolios and outcomes. As you invest trust in positive outcomes, you will throw your energies at the next obstacle that comes your way, and getting the same good results. A positive, self-fulfilling, upward spiral is now in place. The self-fulfilling aspect underlying your trust in positive or negative outcomes is so crucial, and yet so commonly overlooked, that I really cannot emphasise it enough.

I am basically telling you that a lot of your success in life is simply up to your choices. You can choose to believe in negative stuff (and have all that stuff become self-fulfilling for you), or you can choose to believe in positive stuff and have that positive stuff become self-fulfilling for you instead. Since you have to think and choose anyway, you might as well choose to invest in positive beliefs that help you get more of the results you want in your life. Back in the very first chapter, I said that our attitude at the start of a project influences the outcome. Yes, it is true – you may have a great attitude and still be run over by a bus through no choice of your own. Yes, it is true that you have little say or influence over whether a war or earthquake happens where you live. But these events hijacking your success in life are relatively unlikely. In most day-to-day endeavours, the impact of the independent external reality is minimal and it's mostly just about changing your attitude.

It's been documented in all sorts of record-breaking data that once a psychological belief about something thought to be impossible (e.g. certain mountains thought impossible to climb, the impossibility of running a mile in under four minutes) is broken, the floodgates open and the hitherto impossible record is trounced in increasingly irreverent and humiliating ways (e.g. running several miles in a row in under four minutes).

The first, original record-breakers would have had to change their beliefs about themselves in order to succeed. They chose to believe that they could master these challenges, and created a self-fulfilling prophecy.

Many years ago I read a book called *The Luck Factor* by psychologist Richard Wiseman. Wiseman wanted to study luck in a scientific way.

He studied 5,000 self-reported lucky people and 5,000 self-reported *unlucky* people. He found that each group had its own typical attitude and belief system that ended up seeming to create good or bad luck for them. Wiseman then developed a 'luck school', with the aim of teaching some of the unlucky people how to develop better luck through positive attitudes and perspective. When he followed up with them, the formerly unlucky students soon reported a big increase in their luck.

Isn't that a wonderful thing to hear?

You don't have to put your life on hold waiting to win the lottery or for Mr or Mrs Perfect to come knocking at your door. You can change your attitude, choose to believe in yourself, see yourself as wonderful project to invest in, and watch yourself begin to fill the shoes you've been given.

Negative self-belief: *Take Me Out*

I was watching an amusing TV dating programme called *Take Me Out* recently. In this programme, a handsome man chose a pretty woman to go out on a date. Both my wife and I thought the man and woman were well matched in terms of attractiveness, but the female contestant was convinced the man who chose her was out of her league. This was not at all the reality of the situation. A pre-date interview with the man proved that was certainly not what he thought. He was happy with his choice and said he really fancied her.

On the date itself, whenever the man tried to compliment the woman, she couldn't accept it. She found ways to deflect, dismiss or turn his compliments into a joke. This threw the man off his game. As the date progressed it appeared that the woman managed to successfully talk the man out of wanting to be with her. When, at the end, the poor man gave up, saying he didn't think it was worth meeting for a second date, this would have reaffirmed the woman's self-belief that she was not good enough in the first place, or that it 'wasn't meant to be', or that the 'chemistry wasn't there' (when it was obvious to everyone else that they really liked each other at the start) or any other false rationalisation. This woman chose to invest in negative beliefs about herself, which became self-fulfilling.

In short, anxious people tend to remain anxious because they have not fully grasped the crucial importance of the self-fulfilling aspect of success. They are still stuck in the old paradigm that their reality will always be independent of their actions. As such they continue to look for certainties before taking action, seeking risk-free guarantees.

The modern scientific paradigm realises that we are not independent observers of our reality.[10] More often than not we are co-creators of our reality and have a far greater input in our current circumstances than we realise.

As a co-creator of your reality, choose the best attitudes and beliefs to enrich that reality.

If one example from a TV dating show is not enough to convince you of the importance of trusting in yourself and self-belief, I'm going to end this chapter with a couple of formal scientific experiments that illustrate the points made throughout this chapter.

In psychology, *experimenter expectancy effects* (the influence that a researcher can exert on the outcome of a research investigation) have been well documented. In one experiment,[11] a psychologist (R. Rosenthal) had two groups of students test rats, wrongly informing them that the rats were specially bred to be 'maze dull' or 'maze bright'.

---

10. Famous studies on light particles reveal that light will act as either a particle or as a wave depending on how the observer sees this reality.
11. Rosenthal, R and Fode, K 1963, 'The effect of experimenter bias on performance of the albino rat', *Behavioral Science*, vol. 8, no. 3, pp. 183–89.

In reality, all the rats were standard lab rats, and were randomly assigned the 'dull' and 'bright' conditions. The results showed that the rats *labelled* as 'bright' learned the mazes more quickly than those labelled as 'dull'. Apparently, students had unconsciously influenced the performance of their rats, depending on what they had been told. So even rats can perform better if someone believes in them!

Rosenthal reasoned that a similar effect might occur with teachers' expectations of student performance. Rosenthal and Jacobson tested children at Oak School with an IQ test – the Tests of General Ability (TOGA) – at the beginning of the school year to obtain a baseline reading of their IQ before the experiment. Then eighteen teachers at the school were informed of the students in their classes who had obtained scores in the top 20 percent of this test. These students were ready to realise their potential, according to their test scores. What the teachers didn't know is that students were placed on the 'ready to bloom' lists completely at random. There was no difference between these students and other students whose names were not on the lists. At the end of the school year, all students were once again tested with the same TOGA test. Students who had been labelled 'ready to bloom' showed much greater gains than those who had not been labelled in this way.

Rosenthal and Jacobson's results powerfully demonstrate the point. Students believed to be on the verge of great academic success performed in accordance with these expectations; students who weren't labelled this way did not.[12]

I once attended a workshop on self-esteem in which the lecturer related the case of a teacher who was given a class full of very difficult pupils. The teacher started off being very gentle and very patient with the pupils but found she was not succeeding in improving their academic

12. Rosenthal, R and Jacobson, L 1963, 'Teachers' expectancies: Determinants of pupils' IQ gains', *Psychological Reports*, vol. 19, pp. 115–18.

performance. One day, finding herself at the limits of her patience, she went to principal's office to check the files on her pupils, to see if they had any learning difficulties. She found the pupils' IQ scores next to their names. To her surprise, the worst offender in her class had the highest IQ (a score of 148). The teacher reconsidered her approach to her pupils and assumed the poor performance must have been due to her unchallenging and unstimulating teaching style, which made her pupils bored. She became tougher with them, firmer with her deadlines and set them plenty of work. Pupils' listening skills improved and they started to work harder. The class went on to do very well. At a party later on, the principal of the school asked the teacher the secret of her success. The teacher finally admitted that she had sneaked a look at her pupils' files while he was away, saw their IQ scores, and that's what made her reconsider her attitude to them. The principal laughed – it was not the pupils' IQ scores he had listed next to their names, it was their locker numbers!

The teacher believed that the pupils had the potential to perform well. She laid down 'large shoes' for them to step into and fill, and she believed they could fill these shoes with their potential. They did, and you can do too.

Building more faith and trust in yourself

Anxiety is essentially about fear of *pain in the future*. Most anxious people will say that they are coping in the present, it's just that they don't trust themselves to continue coping in the same way into the future. In essence they don't trust their future selves to be as committed or capable in dealing with their problems as they do with their present-day selves.

For instance, many people who have already had successes in dating, job interviews or meetings under their belt will still be anxious about future dating or job interviews despite their past track record. They will not think, 'Well, I always manage to cope somehow, so the most rational conclusion must be that I can cope in such events.'

Instead they will tend to think, 'I don't believe I'm good at dating or job interviews and the ten dates or ten interviews that I've gotten in the past must all be a lucky streak which has probably run out now.'

They are unable to see their own positive contribution to their success. They need to be reminded of their own positive contributions and skill sets in dealing with future problems. To experience this, follow the instructions in the Chapter Exercise at the end of this chapter.

Trusting yourself internally

Recently I worked with a young man I will call Matt, who had severe food phobias. I asked Matt what specifically prevented him from eating the foods he wanted to eat. He mentioned that his throat would start to gag and reject the food, regardless of his intention to eat the food, which he intellectually knew was harmless.

In simple terms we have one part of Matt that trusts that food is harmless, and another part that does not trust the food and considers it an ongoing threat. These two parts are in opposition to each other.

I like to work with metaphors a lot in therapy, adopting and voicing the feelings of different parts out loud. With a little bit of exploring, it soon became apparent that the mistrustful part was effectively saying, 'Why should I trust you to eat food without throwing up? I mean, let's look at your past track record of failures. It doesn't exactly inspire me with confidence, does it?'

I worked with the mistrustful part to restore confidence, which is actually a key part of getting any permanent change, and with that in place, I could proceed with the rest of my therapeutic techniques without any resistance. At the end of the session Matt calmly took an apple in his hand, bit into it (something he had never managed to do before in his life) and sat there in disbelief as he realised his system was not going to gag any more, because it trusted him to be able to eat and digest food normally. Matt has since sent me updates regaling me of the other foods he is trying.

I have literally many hundreds of cases similar to this, where I consider the lynchpin of success to have been first negotiating and establishing trust between the conscious and subconscious minds. It brings home to me the point that lasting faith and trust in yourself really need to be established internally first, and then can be expressed outwards into the wider world.

I used the analogy of the conscious mind and subconscious mind being in a relationship together, and like all relationships, sometimes there are misunderstandings and breakdowns in communication, leading to a hostile or unhealthy inner relationship that spills over into somatic complaints, insecurity, doubt, worry and obsessive thoughts.

If you do not feel in alignment about your goals or feel as if another part of you is dragging you down or sabotaging you in some way, then that is very likely because a part of your subconscious mind does not trust you to achieve your goals.

In summary

> Simply put, the only difference between a confident person and an unconfident person is the *type of trust* they invest in.

> Anxious, unconfident people trust that *negative* outcomes will largely happen. Confident people trust that *positive* outcomes will largely happen.

> Confident people mostly envision a virtual reality where they may have setbacks but will ultimately achieve their goals. They assume it's just a matter of *when* they get good results, not *if*. Anxious people

mostly envision a virtual reality where the end goal is not being realised due to overwhelming obstacles. They tend to get stuck as the 'what *if*' stage.

> Whichever virtual scenario you envision usually ends up becoming self-fulfilling for you.

> Self-belief and self-trust unleashes massive action, which will erode obstacles and lead to impressive results. Poor self-belief and self-trust leads to inhibited, tentative, uncommitted action that makes a smaller impact and leads to less impressive results.

> The self-fulfilling aspect underlying your trust in positive or negative outcomes is crucial and yet so commonly overlooked.

> The modern science paradigm realises that we are not independent of our reality, but that we are co-creators of our reality. As a co-creator of your reality, choose the best attitudes and beliefs that will enrich your reality.

> Getting your subconscious mind to trust your conscious mind, and vice versa, leads to a deep, grassroots level of trust in yourself.

CHAPTER EXERCISE – BUILDING TRUST IN SELF

If anxiety (fear of future harm) is based on not trusting your future self to perform as well as you are now, then you need to understand your future self better, so you can be reassured about his/her confidence to deal with future problems.

So, cast your mind to a concern you have in the future.

For instance, if the present-day you is living on 15 November, and the event you are worried about is scheduled to take place 10 January, then you need to meet your 'January' self to evaluate how well he/she will cope with that event.

Imagine your January self appearing in front of you. As you look at him/her, listen to my words and rest assured that your future self is just as dedicated and committed to coping with your problems as you are committed to coping with your problems in the now.

You are the same person with the same values and commitment to standards.

In fact, if anything, your future self is a little bit older and wiser than the current you. Your future self will reassure you that whatever is important for you to check on and go over will be just as important for him/her when the time comes. Your future self reminds you to stop worrying about what might turn up unexpectedly in the future because he/she is there to handle it for you.

Your future self tells you to just focus on dealing with your problems in the present, where you already have your hands full, and to let your future self worry about his/her problems when and if they happen on his/her 'watch'.

Trust your future self will be there to deal with your future concerns.

See your future self assessing the situation accordingly, then taking appropriate action, doing everything that needs to be done. Because your future self is just as committed as you to your high standards for, e.g. pleasing your customers or writing the best report, you know that if he/she does not have the answers directly, they will go about finding someone who does. Either way, the future problems will be resolved. Trust that you are in safe hands.

Your future self reminds you that:

> There have been many times in the past when you felt out of your league and then you surprised yourself and exceeded your expectations. This is going to be another one of them, so have faith.

> Even if you did not perform well initially in the past, when you first encountered this type of problem, you can learn to perform better in the future. It's not set in stone. You have an adaptable 'plastic' brain that can learn, update and upgrade itself. Past performance is not an indicator of future results.

> Others in similar situations have made it and they are humans – not aliens – and fundamentally no different to you. The success club is open to all.
> Trust in an underlying process at work, a process where you are constantly learning and adapting. You do not need all the answers at the outset. Believe that you will find them on the way.

CHAPTER 6: STATE MANAGEMENT

If you do not conquer self, you will be conquered by self.

– Napoleon Hill

All the approaches I have recommended so far in this book – stepping back, seeing the bigger picture, persevering, rolling with the hard times, focusing on a longer goal – all require you to keep, to one degree or another, a cool enough head to endure your current adversity. If you cannot keep a cool head and manage your emotional state, then you will be compromising your efforts in all these areas and will end up undoing a lot of your progress towards your goals. You might even give up on your goal if you can't handle the perceived stress from it.

If you cannot manage your anger, then you will alienate your customers or colleagues and end up burning bridges you cannot afford to lose.

If you cannot manage your fear, you will miss out on potentially lucrative contacts, new customers or life-enriching experiences in general.

If you cannot manage your stress and frustration, you will build up intolerable pressure that will hamper your performance or derail you from your goals.

If you cannot manage your hurt and rejection, you will take everything personally and either retreat in injured silence, or lash out inappropriately at people who mean well for you.

If you cannot manage your guilt or shame, you will be paralysed by self-judgement and feel unworthy and undeserving of success.

Simply put – either you master your emotions or they will end up mastering you.

A few months ago I watched a documentary about chimpanzees. The chimps were assessed in many different cognitive, memory and spatial tasks. We know that chimps are physically far stronger and tougher than humans, but these cognitive tests also revealed that chimps were superior to us in other categories, too, sometimes vastly so. The programme raised the question that, if chimps were so superior to us on many levels, why did *Homo sapiens* dominate chimps, rather than the other way around? What special advantage did we have that made such a difference? The programme concluded that one of the main reasons was that humans developed a measure of emotional regulation that chimps did not. Chimps would work together on hunting trips, but as soon as prey was killed, their cooperation would degenerate and it was back to everyone out for themselves.

Humans, on the other hand, would take food home for other members of the group in exchange for other benefits, or look after older or sicker members without anything to be gained. As humans, we had better social cooperation. We could empathise with each other better, which meant we could get on with each other, putting aside personal matters for the sake of group cohesion. We could seek, for example, to address our differences in a formal way (through the law) without ripping apart the social fabric of our group.

Social cooperation allowed us to live together in more populated, closely packed tribes, which in turn allowed us to benefit from all the different specialisations and divisions of labour that individual members of the group could offer (which would end up enhancing the survival prospects of all members of the group as a whole).

Occasionally, while I am driving, another reckless or impatient driver may cut into my path in a dangerous way. In that moment I might experience a surge of anger and feel like punching the driver. But other factors would kick in, too, which can modulate my response.

Suppose, for instance, that one of my patients is a Mafia boss, like Tony Soprano. Tony is in the passenger seat when I'm driving and witnesses the incident in which the reckless driver cuts me off. An hour later, Tony takes me aside and says he has a surprise for me. He leads me into an underground room, where I see the reckless driver blindfolded and tied up on a chair.

Tony proudly presents me with a baseball bat and informs me that he followed the driver home and kidnapped him. There were no witnesses so there would be no consequences to harming him. 'Enjoy,' Tony says. 'This can't come back to you in any way.'

Free from any fear of punishment, how many of us would actually be pleased at this prospect? Like, I imagine, most people, I would be aghast and horrified. I would quickly untie the driver, apologise profusely for his experience and calmly explain to Tony that this is not what I meant during my little surge of road rage.

It is one thing to fantasise in the moment about hurting someone who has crossed me, and quite another to see the human being and want to carry out revenge for a trivial matter, after the fact. My socialised, civilised, moral brain would reason with my ego and it would win.

If we all gave in to our whims all the time, we would never have reached this stage of our civilisation. Life would be lawless and chaotic. However, poor emotional regulation is still rife and causing untold damage everywhere around us, from relationships and careers, to social alliances and football matches. We still have a long way to go.

Mastering your emotions

Please note that I am not advocating you become an emotionless robot or a Vulcan (for fans of *Star Trek*). You can still feel the feelings you feel – indeed, you should be passionate about the positive and healthy pursuits in your life. But you can feel what you feel and still have more choice over your responses. You can accept and be 'present' with them without actually giving yourself over to them.

Since I am in a science fiction frame of mind, remember the lesson of Darth Vadar in *Star Wars,* who gave in to his anger – it led him to the Dark Side.

It's not the absence of emotions I am aiming for, but their management. And by the way, just in case you think that advising people to manage their emotions would be easy for me to say because, as a psychologist, I am probably less emotional by nature, you could not be further from the truth. By nature, I am a hothead. I come from a very fiery and emotional culture. My hometown in Crete, Greece, is a bit like Sicily, complete with the long history of vendettas and people being quick to anger in defending their honour. I got into a lot of scraps at school.

Despite my natural temperament, I aspire to keep a cool head. Sometimes stress or tiredness will sneak up on me and I will reply straight from the emotional part of my brain, but I can only work with the design and machinery I've been given. On the whole I can definitely say, with pride, that I manage to keep my cool far more than I lose it. It is totally possible to make big changes even if you consider yourself to be emotionally volatile.

To manage your emotions, you will have to understand and work with the main powerhouse of your emotional arousal – your *amygdala.*

The amygdala

You have a thinking, rational brain (the pre-frontal cortex, or the area around your forehead), and you have a more primitive, emotionally reactive brain (the amygdala – an almond-shaped part of your brain located somewhere in the middle). It's as if you have a Pentium 200 super-processor in your forehead and a lousy, outdated Pentium 0.5 in the middle.

When you are calm and collected, you engage your thinking brain. If you encounter a small problem, you can quickly analyse the different aspects and perspectives involved, empathise with different points of view, articulate your thoughts to others, and take on board their ideas in turn. You can see the ambiguities present and you can see a range of responses (solutions, humour, lateral-thinking and creative ways around it). No wonder we humans have conquered the problems thrown at us in our evolution so far, with such a powerful tool!

On the other hand when you are upset, enraged, frustrated, hurt, sad or in lust, these strong emotions will activate the limbic system, which actually has the power to shut down your thinking brain and divert processing to the simpler amygdala instead.

When the amygdala takes over and you fall back on a Pentium 0.5 processor instead of a Pentium 200, you will see things in a very limited, all or nothing, black or white way. We start thinking in terms of friend or foe – either people support us unconditionally or they constitute part of our problem. There is no middle ground. We fail to see ambiguities and other. Instead we experience a narrowing of focus and tunnel vision around one point. We lose our empathy and our humour in the process.

Not only are we processing information poorly in this situation, but we also have difficulty articulating it to ourselves and others, so when we most need help, we are least able to convey it. As blood flow is being diverted away from neurones in the frontal lobe, speech and verbal areas in the temporal lobes (and goes instead to the heart and muscles), our IQ actually plummets and we become stupider, more short-sighted, more intransigent, unresourceful and belligerent.

Why on earth would our body conspire to dumb us down in our times of greatest need?

The answer goes a little bit like this.

Imagine you are a primitive stone-age human. There you are in the savannah, answering a call of nature, when suddenly you see and hear a rustle in the bushes nearby. Immediately your body responds with a massive chemical chain reaction, preparing you body to flee (avoidance is the preferred option), or freeze and play dead, or fight off the new threat. Your heart starts beating madly, adrenaline courses in your veins, your mouth goes dry, sweat breaks out on your brow, your eyes dilate, your vision narrows down on the point of immediate urgency, your muscles tense, ready to explode into flight or into a mad fighting frenzy. You turn to face the dreaded predator, perhaps a massive bear or another hostile caveman, and out pops ... a squirrel.

You sigh in relief.

Does your system say to itself, 'Ah, silly me. All that worry and it was just a squirrel. Next time the bush rustles, I will take a deep breath, adopt a more philosophical frame of mind and remind myself not to jump to conclusions. It could be a lion, but it equally could be a harmless squirrel, so I won't panic.' (In short, pretty much all the advice that modern doctors, psychologists, therapists and coaches would advise you to adopt.)

No. Your system aims to turn on the exact same startle and alarm response every time, and at that point in our evolution, it would have been appropriate to do so. Your defence system does not care about looking silly or sheepish. It does not care if a false scare is the price of safety and prudence. Your survival is more important. When your survival is at stake, your system doesn't have time to mess about philosophising and speculating. It needs immediate action in the shortest range of time possible. Every millisecond might be critical to your survival, so anything other than survival systems are considered superfluous and get shut down.

If someone is throwing a punch at you, you do not want to be distracted by irrelevant thoughts like whether you forgot something while shopping or to check your lottery numbers. You need to pinpoint your attention on one thing and one thing only, and that is the immediate threat. Reflexes work far faster than thinking neural networks, so we experience emotional reactions first. Later, we have the luxury of thought to modify them.

Nowadays, of course, things have changed. Mr Pain has gone from being the most valued member of the defence team to the most annoying and outdated. We have gone from needing to operate from our amygdala the majority of the time to now needing to engage it only a minority of the time. But those instincts are still strong inside us.

The trick is to become more discerning about these signals. For instance, there are times when fear and adrenaline may save your life. But most of the time, adrenaline is wasted and being triggered over situations that have nothing to do with actual life or death situations. A life or death situation is someone holding a gun to your head. It is not speaking at a meeting or performing in front of your peer group. But it sure feels like life or death to the person that has such a phobia.

Coping with emotional arousal and stress would require a book on its own to do the topic justice. What I can offer here are some broad tips for managing psychological stress and emotional arousal in general. I will also be focusing on how to not take things personally, because taking things to heart is at the root of a lot of emotional upset today.

Putting the amygdala in its place
There are a number of things you can do to put your amygdala in its place and not fall under its spell:

1. Recognise the amygdala's role and contribution
Whenever I work with couples and relationship counselling, couples will often start off thinking that their partner is their arch enemy and the source of all their problems.

People soon realise that it is not their partner that is the problem, but that they both have a common enemy – their biology. All of the arguments, snapping at each other and tiffs are a result of their amygdala being activated. As mentioned, when the amygdala dominates our processing, we lose empathy – we are unable to hear, process and understand others' feelings, and we each think that the other person is the enemy in our way. That's what happens, biologically, when two animals square off against each other.

Your partner is (usually) your friend. You love them and they love you. What gets in the way is stress, tiredness and other factors, which lead to the amygdala being activated, which then takes over and makes you react in primitive ways.

I also point out to couples that whatever is done or said under the rule of the amygdala should be treated as mitigating circumstances or diminished responsibility. It would be very inaccurate to hold your partner to account for what was said when their Pentium 0.5 processor thought you were a hostile caveperson out to kill them. I know for a fact that I have said things during arguments I did not mean at all – and I *know* about the role the amygdala plays in such situations. In the heat of the moment, thinking goes out of the window.

With a cooler head I know that there is no point arguing or blaming the other person when I am upset, because I cannot truly understand or communicate with them in such a state anyway (and neither can they with me, for that matter). Instead I know that what I am really up against is my own biology.

In these cases, switching away from the perceived enemy (one's partner, friend, family member) to the 'real' enemy is a useful diversion in attention. It means you can move away from just shouting louder at someone you cannot currently empathise with (and who is not in a position to hear you anyway). Instead you can move to where the real action is at – with you – and focus your attention on taking appropriate steps to prevent your amygdala taking over. That requires knowing how to keep a cool head.

2. Keeping a cool head

Under times of stress or fear, you probably already recognise the adrenaline coursing through your body, making your heart beat faster, your mouth dry, your palms sweaty, etc. I would now also like you to recognise your amygdala pathway in a similar way now.

Think of your amygdala as sitting at the top of a jackpot. Any strong emotion means the emotional current is working its way up to the amygdala, just like mercury up a thermometer, until it finally hits the jackpot, at which point the amygdala takes over and shuts down your thinking brain. Then your IQ will plummet and you will likely be too stupid to solve the problem you need to solve. You will just end up making a worse mess of it.

As soon as I register the emotional current beginning to work its way up to my amygdala, I know I have a small and decreasing window of opportunity in which to prevent things deteriorating – a limited amount of time to act before I too become stupid and unresourceful, reacting in ever more limited emotional ways. In other words I am in a race against my amygdala, and know I have to act to derail it before it derails me.

I find the best way to do this is to:

> Take a deep breath and literally and physically take one step back.
> Imagine you have stepped out of the stressed 'you', leaving him/her there in front of you, in that position, and that you have stepped into a new more objective and detached space.
> From your place of detachment, acknowledge his or her stress there, in a detached way, without any judgement or analysis (i.e. see yourself in the third person perspective). Just accept it as you would accept the sun overhead or the trees around you
> Once you have accepted his/her feelings, consider what advice would you give to your stressed self. It could be practical advice (e.g. imposing some sort of order and prioritising) or it could be a

handy metaphor such as, 'Imagine the stress is parting around you like Moses parting the waves of the Red Sea.' Anything that works for the stressed you over there will do.

> Step back into the stressed you and feel yourself receiving that advice or support. Take it on board and feel the difference in your emotional state now.

> If the change is sufficient, enjoy it. If not, repeat the process, considering what else is needed here.

Mole and Badger

This short story is very useful for dealing with anger and frustration

Mole was driving along a motorway with his friend, Badger. Mole was enjoying the drive and feeling good about the world until another car, driven by Rat, cut aggressively and dangerously in front of him.

Mole was furious. He put his foot on the accelerator and chased Rat, flashing, hooting and gesticulating. Mole was shouting, cursing and purple with rage. Rat simply laughed to himself, made a rude gesture with his fingers, and accelerated away.

Mole was quite upset for the next hour. His day was totally spoilt. He felt frustrated and inadequate, as if his whole sense of mastery had been called into question. He had been challenged and come off second-best.

Badger noticed his friend's behaviour but had chosen to say nothing for the time being. He waited until the time was right.

Finally Mole turned and said to him, 'That sort of driver makes me so angry.'

Badger replied, 'Forgive me, but I'm really curious. Why exactly did you allow yourself to get angry because of what another driver did?'

Mole was speechless. He had expected support. 'What do you mean?' he exclaimed.

Badger said, 'What that other person did *was simply information about him*. How you responded is information about you. How exactly did *you make yourself* angry as a response to the other driver's behaviour?'

So it was that Mole began to realise he could choose his response to different situations. He could get angry if he wished, or stay calm and dismiss someone else's behaviour as information about them. It didn't have to affect him.

After that Mole began to enjoy his driving a lot more. Badger felt a lot safer in Mole's car, and Mole's wife noticed her husband was much less stressed and aggressive.

One day, Mole told Badger he'd found a great quote in a book he was reading: *No one pressed your hot buttons. You just left your control panel open.*

'That's what I used to do,' Mole said, stressing the *used to*.[13]

3. Don't take things personally

Taking things personally means you have cast your net of cause and effect over a very small area and generalised to the whole from just a small piece. It's like having a blindfold on, touching the trunk of an elephant and being convinced you are holding a python.

Once we take things personally, we start to make all sorts of inaccurate attributions, such as those mentioned earlier in Chapter 1, and we end up accusing some poor innocent person of attacking us in the bargain.

Remember – your amygdala is predisposed to take things personally. It takes the rustle in the bushes personally. It makes everything that goes on around you about you.

If you ever walk near little animals in the park, they will almost always flee from you, regardless of your neutral or friendly intent. They

13. Grinder, M 1991, *Righting the Educational Conveyor Belt*, Metamorphous Press, Portland.

assume everything that is bigger than them is out to get them. They see themselves as the centre of the universe, with every action potentially related to them in some way.

The amygdala will take things personally first, then think and pick up the pieces later, if it even bothers to do that. The instinct to take things personally is the default setting. Recognising this tendency, you can now stand back and question your feelings of personalisation. Just because it feels personal to you, does not mean it is about you. Not everything that happens to you is about you – in fact, it rarely is.

The Cookie Thief by Valerie Cox

Here is a wonderful poem I came across that beautifully illustrates our tendency to make assumptions and therefore read a situation completely wrong.

A woman was waiting at an airport one night,
With several long hours before her flight.
She hunted for a book in the airport shops.
Bought a bag of cookies and found a place to drop.
She was engrossed in her book but happened to see,
That the man sitting beside her, as bold as could be,
Grabbed a cookie or two from the bag in between,
Which she tried to ignore to avoid a scene.
So she munched the cookies and watched the clock,
As the gutsy cookie thief diminished her stock.
She was getting more irritated as the minutes ticked by,
Thinking, 'If I wasn't so nice, I would blacken his eye.'
With each cookie she took, he took one too,
When only one was left, she wondered what he would do.
With a smile on his face, and a nervous laugh,
He took the last cookie and broke it in half.
He offered her half, and as he ate the other,

She snatched it from him and thought, 'Oh, brother.
This guy has some nerve and he's also rude,
Why he didn't even show any gratitude!'
She had never known when she had been so galled,
And sighed with relief when her flight was called.
She gathered her belongings and headed to the gate,
Refusing to look back at the thieving ingrate.
She boarded the plane, and sank in her seat,
Then she sought her book, which was almost complete.
As she reached in her baggage, she gasped with surprise,
There was her bag of cookies, in front of her eyes.
If mine are here, she moaned in despair,
The others were his, and he tried to share.
Too late to apologise, she realised with grief,
That she was the rude one, the ingrate, the thief.

4. Distinguishing between good worry and bad worry

The real trick is to respect the underlying useful message the amygdala is trying to communicate, without being sidetracked by the *way* the message is conveyed. In this sense there is a distinction between good worry and bad worry. *Good worry* is a reminder for a call to action and leads to solution-focused behaviour. *Bad worry* leads to complaining, blaming, judging and pointless analysis.

For instance, I might feel a dose of worry hit me when I glance at my calendar and a little voice inside says, 'Felix, if you don't sort out your tax return soon, you will pay a fine completely needlessly. C'mon, time is running out.'

I treat this little voice like an inner personal assistant. In this case, I respond with, 'Good point, let me check my schedule, book in some time to complete my tax return and get it out of the way.' The problem is resolved without any need for any further expenditure of energy.

In contrast, using the same analogy, bad worry would lead to a response along the lines of, 'Why wasn't I more punctual again with my tax return again this year? Why can't I just be more organised? Who's to blame for not teaching me how to be more punctual? Who did I inherit disorganisation from, and why were they so disorganised in the first place?', etc, etc.

You'll notice that none of these latter responses relate to any form of solution to help me achieve my goal. Instead the focus of attention shifts my energy towards pointless speculation and distractions and away from the actual task at hand.

To make matters worse, the more you analyse, judge and blame in response to your problems, the more emotional you will become – the more angry, frustrated, guilty or sad you will feel. Often people then become overwhelmed by these emotions and end up becoming completely derailed and disconnected from any sort of solution-focused thinking.

Analysis has a seductive myth around it: '*If only* I could just understand *why* I am this way, then everything will magically sort itself out.' I have seen countless people unhelpfully analyse their problems and not actually do anything useful about them. For me, as an observer, it often seems as if such people believe in a fantasy that there is the existence of *one super answer* that will immediately dispel their problem, that if only they could analyse the situation a little bit more, they would end up finally capturing that answer.

The truth is, there is rarely a 'super answer' to your problem behaviour. All too often the answers tend to be mundane and simple, and we are less interesting and dramatic than we believe we are. We act in certain ways mostly due to a little bit of genetics, a little bit of personality traits, a little bit of learned behaviour, such as unhelpful habits, and a little bit of the amygdala doing its job in the only way it knows how. There isn't always a deep and sexy answer, or a Holy Grail waiting to be discovered.

No doubt some of these people are engaging in analysis as an excuse to avoid knuckling down to the less-than-desirable job at hand, instead taking a more appealing intellectual road trip to find their answers. But often a problem will not be solved unless you roll up your sleeves and get stuck in. Clever little intellectual escapades and excuses will not lead to your homework being done, your reports being written, your room or house being tidied up, your body being exercised, your text books being read.

To summarise on this point – if you are going to worry, be a good worrier, and make sure your attention and responses are always solution-focused.

The glowing red ball

There are an infinite number of creative ways by which you can manage your state. You have to find an approach that suits and works for you, but give your creativity free rein!

For instance, I was working with a client, whom I'll call Ben, for anger management. Rather than using the technique mentioned previously, involving physically stepping into new locations and perspectives, we experimented with a variation that went like this.

Felix: OK, Ben, just close your eyes for a moment and go inside … get in touch with that anger you felt on that evening. Let me know when you feel it.

Ben: [nods his head]

Felix: Good. Now just flow that anger down your right arm to your palm, until all of it is there. Let me know when that's done.

Ben: [nods his head]

Felix: Describe to me what you are experiencing now on that right palm.

Ben: It's like a red ball.

Felix: A red ball. And is this red ball still or moving?

Ben: It's swirling fast

Felix: So its got a lot of energy driving it, right?

Ben: Yes.

Felix: Just allow the ball to keep swirling faster and faster as much as it needs to in order to ride through its course of action or until it's spent.

Ben: OK, it's stopped moving now.

Felix: Good. Now that it's stopped moving, imagine you could send a line of communication to this part, to say, 'Hey, what's up?'

Ben: *[gets in touch with the real underlying issue of anger rather than the surface problem]*

Felix: Now that we know what that part was actually angry about … what do you think that part wants in order to be more at peace with things?

Ben: *[tunes back in and get some feedback]*

Felix: So what this part of you needs is for you to do x, y and z. And are you prepared to do all those things?

Ben: Yes.

Felix: So you commit to do these things and you also know *how* to do them?

Ben: Yes.

Felix: So can you just go ahead and do them now, or is there any other obstacle that we need to address first?

Ben: No, I can get on and do them.

As you have seen, it's common for me to get my patients to have dialogues with metaphorical parts of themselves. In the process, the unmet needs leading to anger are acknowledged, validated and addressed in a constructive way. Simple little techniques can be surprisingly powerful in helping people to manage their state, because they derail or interrupt the habitual channels of expression and get the person to experience the emotion in new ways. It doesn't matter whether you see a spinning red ball, a little monster, a sharp spike, or whatever. Experiment with some of the same stages mentioned here, and notice how it can really change your old experience.

In summary

> If you cannot keep a cool head and manage your emotional state, you will be compromising your development of resilience and the other qualities described in previous chapters.

> You might give up on your otherwise achievable goal wholesale if you cannot handle the perceived stress around it.

> Either you master your emotions or they will end up mastering you.

> Poor emotional regulation is rife and causes untold damage in relationships, jobs, etc.

> The amygdala is the powerhouse of fear.

> When we remain cool and level-headed we operate with our thinking brain – our prefrontal cortex (akin to a Pentium 200). When we are emotional or stressed, we start operating more from the amygdala (akin to a Pentium 0.5 and usually inadequate for the problems we need to solve). We need to recognise the amygdala's role and contribution to our behaviour.

> As we become more stressed or emotional, we have a decreasing, small window of opportunity to prevent the amygdala from taking over.

> We can step back and take calming action so that you don't give in to the amygdale by practising:

- keeping a cool head
- not taking things personally
- distinguishing between good worry and bad worry.

CHAPTER EXERCISE – FOCUSING ON THE AUTHENTIC SELF

I would like to share with you a hugely powerful new perspective that came to me intuitively one day, and which has helped many of my clients form new meanings about their relationships and experiences in their life.

Step 1. Pick a person you have a current conflict with (family members, colleague, partner) and imagine they are with you.

Step 2. The place where you are standing and looking out at this person we will call 'first position'. Now imagine they are standing directly in front of you – in a place we will call 'second position'. Acknowledge your feelings towards them without any judgement. Just 'honour' your feelings, so to speak. It's likely that you feel hurt, angry, sad or guilty, because of the meanings you have made about their behaviour towards you. In order for you to feel hurt and affected by them in some way, you must have taken their behaviour to heart in some fashion, i.e. you have taken their behaviour personally.

Step 3. Now I would like to you to make a distinction between the 'physical' person you see before you (note one can do this exercise for deceased people, too), and what I call their *authentic self*.

By way of analogy, supposing you and I were lifelong friends and you knew me as a good and kind person. Then, only in the last year of my life, I developed paranoid schizophrenia and Tourette's Syndrome, so that whenever you came to my house to help me I would be shouting and insulting you. If a friend of yours accompanied you and had never met me before, they might say, 'What are you doing with Felix? He's so horrible to you. You should stop seeing him.' To which you might reply, 'Hey, that's not the real Felix. That is the disease talking. The real Felix is my friend and a good man. That's the Felix I am helping here.'

If you agree with this sentiment then you have agreed the physical or historic me is not the real me. The real me may not exist in the physical realm anymore, but in some sort of alternative universe or parallel reality. Nevertheless it represents a truer version of me than this physical shell.

Once you accept this principle, I would like you to extend it to *everyone* who has hurt you. They may not have a very obvious mental disease like schizophrenia, but they will have other mental viruses taking over, caused by their upbringing, genetics, traumas, culture, unique experiences and defences – stuff that gets in the way and takes over their authentic expression.

To put it another way, every puppy I have ever met is affectionate and loving. One could say that by nature puppies are loving and affectionate. But if you take any puppy, put it in a cage with blaring music and torture it, it will start biting. To say that this puppy is horrible would not be doing justice to its authentic nature. The puppy has been traumatised and damaged, but that does not represent its authentic nature.

Step 4. Once you have accepted the notion of an authentic self, which in a strange way represents a truer version of the person in front of you, imagine their authentic self stepping out and standing a little to their side – which we will call 'third position'. I tend to imagine this like one of those special effects we see in movies, a character who is invisible to everyone else but the audience or the protagonist of the film.

The authentic self is free from all the filters of gender, culture, traumas, bigotry, ego, pride. It's as if it operates from the level of the soul, rather than the personality.

Step 5. Step into the 'third position', the authentic self of the person you had a conflict with. Tune into what they would really feel towards you, the person back there at first position, if they were fully free and able to do so. I like to imagine that the authentic self would always take full responsibility for their physical self's actions, offer an unreserved apology, and express how they actually feel towards us.

In the shoes of this person's authentic self, express and convey such feelings towards the 'you' there in the first position.

Step 6. Step back into yourself in first position and receive the message from the other person's authentic self. Notice how that feels.

Step 7. Now you have a choice regarding to whom you will listen. Would you rather listen to the inaccurate message of the physical or historic person (e.g. Felix with schizophrenia, in the second position) or the authentic version in the third position, who is offering you a true message of what the person feels, if only they could express it?

If you are hurt by your parent's lack of acknowledgement for your achievements, imagine your authentic parents standing nearby, saying, 'Don't listen to them, listen to us. We are so proud of you and will always love you.'

If you are hurt by your partner's actions, imagine his/her authentic self standing next to them saying, 'Sorry, he/she is hurt and gets into their defensive mode. They do love you very much but find it difficult to say that to you directly. He/she will try and do that in other ways.'

The next time you are driving and someone cuts into your way, imagine the authentic self sitting next to them, raising their hands apologetically, adding, 'We are so sorry, it's his ego. It goes with the job and the car. We are trying to work on it but it's really difficult and we apologise for the fallout to innocent bystanders.'

It always brings a smile to my face when I picture that.

CHAPTER 7: THE HERO'S JOURNEY

If you want the rainbow, you've got to put up with the rain

– Jimmy Durante

The chapters so far have given you specific insights and tools by which to develop your resilience. Your training is largely done.

As I am a fan of looking for the big picture perspective, this chapter is less about offering you techniques, and more about adding an expanded element of a spiritual perspective. By spiritual perspective, I am referring to a sense of a greater purpose, meaning, consciousness or intelligence working behind the scenes.

Why bother to add a spiritual perspective, you may ask, especially if there is no hard proof of the existence of any higher purpose in your life?

Well, firstly, numerous studies show that people with spiritual beliefs are more robust and resilient, recovering from adversity quicker, than those who do not subscribe to such beliefs. The choice of adopting spiritual beliefs leads to a definite positive impact on their life.[14]

Secondly, even if such people are deluded and there is no God or greater intelligence as such, we can still improve our lives by acting 'as if' there were meaning and purpose present in our existence. The very fact of behaving as if there *should be* meaning and purpose actually *creates* meaning and purpose.

14. Scott, E 2007, 'Spirituality and Mental Health: Benefits of Spirituality', About.com, 2 November, viewed 13 February 2013, <http://stress.about.com/od/optimismspirituality/a/22307_God_power.htm>

One of the themes mentioned numerous times throughout this book is that there is a self-fulfilling element in our beliefs and in the meaning we ascribe to things. If we choose to believe in something spiritual and assign meaning to it, it will become meaningful to us, and we will in turn have 'created' something in our lives, because we will be acting from the perspective of the purpose that we have created. It is possible, therefore, to be an atheist and a spiritual person.

Journey, not destination

As you have probably surmised by now, you are embarking on a process – a journey of development. Sometimes we get so focused on the destination that we forget to appreciate the journey, which is usually more important.

If you are a parent, your 'destination' for your children might be to help them become well educated, find good jobs and marry. But it's more than just ticking those boxes. I've met parents who have become fixated on getting their children to follow a very defined path – these parents may want their children to go to a specific school, followed by a specific university, followed by employment with a particular company. I often remind them that they are getting too focused and rigid about the details. Whether their children get into that good university or that other good university, whether they get that job with that top company or another job with another company, or marry that nice person instead of that other nice person, is all incidental. That's not what really matters.

The journey is far more important – the daily interactions with your children or loved ones, the fun and laughter, the getting to know them, delighting in their uniqueness and development, sharing experiences with them.

If the journey is where the real 'action' is (the knowledge, growth, understanding and development), it stands to reason that our ancestors would have pondered and reflected on this journey too, given it would be such a common universal human experience. What wisdom and insights do they have to advise us?

The hero's journey

Writer Joseph Campbell has studied many different stories from mythology around the world. Subsequently, he thinks that our ancestors may have been trying to advise and prepare us for our own journeys using stories and hero role models.

In his book, *The Hero with a Thousand Faces,* Campbell holds that numerous myths from disparate times and regions share fundamental structures and stages. Broadly speaking, they can be divided into the following acts. Note that many of these acts will be familiar to you because they are staple arechtypes and themes in movies. We are suckers for these particular tropes.

Act 1. The hero *hears a calling.*

This is life sending a call to action for the hero.

The hero might be content in their comfort zone, but life wants them to develop and reach their potential. In modern movies, one often sees the hero happily doing a low-key job when a friend from the past arrives in need, or their ex-General flies in informing them of a national emergency, and the hero's special, untapped skill set is required to fix the problem.

Act 2. The hero *accepts and commits to the calling*.

The hero wrestles with the calling and struggles with fear of losing their current comfort zone. The hero has just got everything set up nice and cosy, but now they are being asked to risk all of that and possibly their lives in pursuit of another ideal. They eventually commit to pursuing that ideal.

Act 3. The hero *crosses a threshold* into some new life 'territory' that forces them to grow and evolve.

The hero needs to be courageous and step out of their comfort zone to face uncertainty.

Act 4. The hero gets assistance or *finds a mentor*.

Once the hero is prepared to face their challenge, life will assist them in their quest.

In mythology, often the gods or their messengers would give them magical weapons or instruments to assist them (e.g. the hero Perseus was given an a reflective shield so he could see Medusa, who would turn him to stone if he looked at her directly, and a magical scythe that could cut through her enchanted hide).

Assistance can also take the form of a mentor to guide you (e.g. Yoda training Luke Skywalker). As it has been said, 'When the student is ready, the teacher appears.' A mentor is someone (or something – like a book!) that appears naturally from the hero having the courage to cross a threshold.

Act 5. The hero *faces the challenge*

In mythology, the challenge was often in the form of a demon or monster. Our demons are not necessarily evil or bad, but simply a type of 'power' that we need to learn to contend with or accept. Often these monsters are a reflection of the hero's own inner shadows.

Act 6. *The demon is transformed* into a resource or advisor.

The hero needs to defeat or tame the dragon. This is typically accomplished by either *developing a special skill*, or *discovering a special resource or tool*.

Act 7. The hero **finds a way to fulfil the calling**.

This is ultimately achieved by creating a new map of the world, which incorporates the growth and discoveries brought about by the journey.

Act 8. The hero returns home **as a transformed or evolved person**.

The hero also shares their knowledge with others in turn.

If you were to see the things you are struggling with in your life in the same way, as part of a growth process – a hero's journey – this could potentially have a massive positive effect and give you undreamed of resilience and endurance.

To illustrate this, read the following two cases – one describes a person who did not have a sense of the hero's journey, and the other one who did.

The case of Gerard

Gerard is a 26-year-old man who came to see me for ongoing depression. Previous experiences with several therapists had helped resolve some of the traumas he had in his life and assisted in other areas, but his depression seemed immune to all attempts at treatment.

Gerard had faced a difficult schooling, recounting how he would be sent out of the class by teachers on an almost daily basis. At the age of 11 he was diagnosed with dyslexia and dyspraxia, which helped explain some of his difficulties in learning and staying engaged in the classroom.

His sister also faced some anxiety issues and Gerard mentioned how he felt guilty about the strain this must have put on his parents.

As I explored the underlying reasons for his depression, Gerard replied with, 'How much more shit do I have to go through?

Everything is one after the other, non-stop. I don't want any more ups or downs.'

Further questioning revealed that Gerard was not angry at himself or anyone else, but with life in general.

Since Gerard had a problem with life, I adopted the same technique as I would in any couples counselling session. I asked Gerard to imagine the personification of Life, if it could be invited into our session to stand opposite him. I asked Gerard to consider if he had one message that he could convey to Life that would epitomise how he felt he'd been treated, what that message would be.

Gerard replied with, 'For God's sake, stop it already, I've had enough. I don't have any fight left. Give me and my family a break.' Gerard also added that, despite coming from a Jewish background, he did not believe in religion because of the stress his family had been put through.

From Gerard's reply, it was obvious that he was feeling victimised and taking things personally. He was at the *effect* side of the equation, rather than the *at cause* side, the 'creator position' (see Chapter 2).

I then asked Gerard to imagine Life replying to him, and saying something along the lines of, 'I'm really sorry. I know this comes across as me picking on you, but I promise it's not. No one is out to punish you or your family. I know it feels like that, but my aim is not to give you a problem-free life but for you to *learn lessons*. I'm trying to get across a very important life lesson that you're just not getting, and because you are not getting it, you are taking it personally. Sometimes out of necessity the lessons are hard, but they are never malicious or designed to hurt, even though they may seem that way.'

Gerard took that in, but then replied, 'How much more crap

do I need to have to be a stronger person? I would think I'd be strong enough by now, going through all this.'

I pointed out to Gerard that he was still taking it personally and feeling picked on. I added that, from my own experience, whenever I took the same position towards Life and said the same things – 'Life, I have had enough, I'm protesting, I deserve a break, I'm angry with you and don't agree with your plan for me, I would like it easier' – I have always felt that Life would say back to me, 'You're still not getting it! When you can accept what you are getting and can see the good in it, it will transform everything. Right now you are stuck because you are not learning. You are just complaining that you don't like my lesson format and that you would like to experience it in a simpler way. You want the benefit of the lesson without the cost of the lesson. I'm trying to turn you into a hero, and you would like to be a hero, but you are protesting about *how* I'm trying to turn you into a hero.'

I gave Gerard an analogy with martial arts, explaining that it's a bit like saying, 'I want a black belt in karate so I can feel more confident and protect myself or my family, but I don't want to put in all the hours, spar with anyone who could hurt me, or get any bruises or punches. I just want to download the skills like Neo in the Matrix without any of the usual hard work or striving.'

Once Gerard started seeing his life more in terms of a hero's journey, his mood increased considerably. He started feeling hopeful again (and hope is an antidote for depression).

Hope

In fact, hope is such an important consideration in building resilience that I need to take a time-out here to talk a bit more about it.

If we have hope we will always remain optimistic, positive that we can succeed in some form or another, even when the current avenues we are trying to venture forth in seem blocked.

By definition, hope operates in a context of uncertainty with regard to success. If there was certainty of success, there would be no hope, just guarantees, which is what a lot of people get stuck waiting around for. The whole point about experiencing uncertainty is that uncertainty compels you to rely and trust in yourself (and in Life) to succeed.

Once you rely on and trust in yourself, you will actually start getting things done and seeing results. Your confidence will develop and you will grow as a person. You will become more philosophical in the face of uncertainty and 'not knowing' will no longer hold the same power to affect you.

In your moments of weakness, you might beg and implore life to make it easy for you and hand you the answers on a plate, without any anxious striving on your part. But Life loves you too much to cheat you out of essential, character-building lessons and later on you will be glad that it didn't cave in to your demands. For instance, if you were handed a ready-made business by a rich relative, you would not appreciate it as much as if you built up that business by yourself. You would always feel cheated and unworthy – 'Well, I didn't really earn it, it was given to me.'

Confidence comes from having your back to the wall, not knowing how you will succeed, but being determined to do so. It's when you find yourself overcoming obstacles that you had no idea how you would tackle at first. The most rewarding things you do in life are often the ones that look like they cannot be done.

So cultivating hope is a result of being free to experience uncertainty. Uncertainty tests you. Having guarantees would be like always knowing the answers to the test ahead of time. There would essentially be no test or problems or need to choose. Yet it is in the testing that you come to know your true potential and grow in confidence.

The case of Viktor Frankl

Previously, Gerard mentioned how he stopped believing in God because of the troubles his family had been through. While it is true that his parents experienced a lot of stress and worry regarding their children, on the other hand, their basic needs for survival and safety were met. There were many options and possibilities for improvement available to them. Now let me compare his case with that of someone who was actually tested within the limits of human endurance and still managed to thrive – the case of Viktor Frankl.

Viktor Frankl was a psychiatrist of Jewish heritage who was forced into a Nazi concentration camp with his family. His wife, brother and uncle all died in the camps. By all accounts, the situation seemed pretty dire to Frankl. He recounted how some prisoners would give up hope and commit suicide by walking into electrified fences.

However, it occurred to Frankl that while most of the prisoners were depressed and miserable about their fate, a small minority (of which he was one) were not only unaffected, but actually seemed to thrive in these conditions. Something had activated unstoppable resilience in these people. No matter how grim things seemed, the hope in these people was unquenchable. Frankl later interviewed some of these individuals and found that were united in a common drive and reason to live. And that reason was the meaning they had assigned to their experience. Their meaning became that they had to live in order to tell the world their story and ensure that it would never happen again. The meaning was about something bigger than their own hardship. It was in service to something greater.

Things must have seemed hopeless for Frankl and his fellow prisoners at the height of the Holocaust, and to stay hopeful when so many others around them were abandoning hope and giving up the will to live required incredible resilience. But their hope was well-founded. Things *did* change for the better. Frankl went on to write his bestselling book, *Man's Search for Meaning*, in which he discussed the importance of finding meaning, and thus a reason to continue living, in all forms of existence, even the most sordid and difficult. In so doing he became a prominent source of inspiration for the humanistic psychology movement, which in turn has helped countless people through their own crises.

I'm pretty sure that, regardless of how bad you feel your situation is, it's unlikely to have been worse than that of Viktor Frankl and even he never lost hope. He survived by choosing a life that gave meaning to his experience. Since we can choose the meanings or 'stories' to describe our lives, we might as well pick a good one that helps us thrive.

Overview

As we take an overview of our developmental process and journey, a number of things become apparent.

The first is that we all need to grow up and (to quote Abba) 'growing up is never easy'. We've got a lot of things stacked up against us at the outset:

> We need to learn to be independent, but we are first 'trained' in being passive, and are used to others being responsible for our needs.

> We want things to be easy, but life can be hard.

> We are drawn to explore the new (neo*philia*) while also psychologically programmed to be uncomfortable with the new (neo*phobia*). So we need to learn new skills, but we fear the unknown.

> We need to act and find our way, but we have no guarantees of success.

> We need to mature and become our own person, but we may have one or more parents determined to make us a clone in their image.

> We need to take responsibility for own needs, weather all the problems life throws at us, find and express our own unique creativity and learn to fend for ourselves.

> It's a big challenge.

> What will make this challenge a lot easier is if we stop complaining and accept from the outset that:

> Life is meant to be difficult. It is not meant to be problem-free to allow you to get what you want, when you want, just because you want it. The aim of life is not to provide you with an indefinite income so you can party and indulge your whims.

> Stop comparing your situation with that of your neighbour, who seems to be having a much easier journey. You have no way of knowing how that will end up for them or for you, or what they have already experienced to get where they are. Focus on your own path.

> Instead of complaining when you encounter a problem, see it as something that is trying to stimulate your growth and development by challenging you. Your problems are your growth opportunities and the building blocks for your character. Life is trying to train you to be the master of your destiny, so you no longer fear what used to hold you back.

> If you feel Life is unfair because you keep experiencing the same problems, it is probably because you are refusing to learn the inherent lesson, and so forcing yourself to keep retaking the same lesson.

> You cannot experience the highs without the lows. The lows give meaning to the highs in the same way that a symphony comprised

of just high notes and no low notes ends up being a cacophony. You need both. Learn to roll with the lows to see where they will take you.

> Life is more than a collection of entries to add to your CV. Focus on the journey and not just the destinations.

> Life seems wasteful and inefficient during times of hardship, but no experience is wasted, even if you cannot make sense of it at the time and it seems unduly malicious. You just have to trust that others like you have been in the same situation and, with the benefit of a long term view, the gains from such experiences will be revealed much later, often after years or decades.

> Embrace your life lessons and Life will stop testing you.

A personal wake-up moment

If you feel like protesting to Life about an experience you are having, saying, 'No, this is too much! I refuse to accept the way this lesson is being presented to me. I want an easier medium without pain, and demand that I should be given this lesson in another format agreeable to me,' then you are effectively stating that you in, all your wisdom, know what is best – when you don't even know the full story.

I would like to share a similar lesson in my life that ran over many years and which finally dispelled these old notions for me. In my early twenties, I was rather a different person that I am today. I was still struggling with different aspects of insecurity, self-worth and people-pleasing issues.

At the age of 22, I met a very pretty waitress a few years older than me, 'Diana', who I started dating. Pretty soon Diana started acting out her own considerable emotional baggage. Her father had married eight different times and Diana had a deep-found insecurity that men would ultimately leave her. She resorted to pre-emptive strikes on me in order to test my love for her. I love a challenge and initially I reasoned that, with enough love, I could win her over and *convince* her that she could trust me, that I was for real.

What I found instead was that the goal posts kept moving! I found myself putting up with more and more unreasonable behaviour. Still, because I was young and relatively inexperienced with long-term relationships I just kept doing the same thing. I had my own insecurities playing out too. I reasoned, 'How else would someone like me get a pretty girl like this?' About a year and a half later, Diana finally broke up with me. I was devastated. I thought, 'Well, as bad as our relationship was, at least there were some scraps of love. I will never find anyone as pretty as this again, who loved me too, even if it was in a very dysfunctional, messed up way.'

Now if God, or Life, or whoever, had appeared in front of me and said, 'Felix, I can see you are suffering and I don't want you to suffer. I tell you what. Here is a magic button. If you press it, I will fix it for you so that you and Diana will get back together forever. Do you want to press it?', then I, like a fool, would have rushed to jam my finger down on the button. All I knew at the time was that I couldn't imagine not feeling this way in the future, and thought that I would be happiest being with Diana forever.

Thank God I wasn't allowed to 'run' my own lessons, because a few years later I met 'Nicole'. Nicole was a quantum leap up from Diana in every way. By then I had also done some work on myself and was better able to accept the kind of 'quality' girlfriend present in Nicole. During this time I even bumped into Diana a few times. Free from the 'glamour' of being in a relationship with her I could see things more objectively and realised that if I had married Diana, we would have ended up divorced pretty quickly. I chalked it up to naivety, but now felt confident that I knew what I was doing.

About a year down the line, however, there was trouble in paradise with Nicole. We were growing apart. She wanted to be an actress, and I was interested in becoming a student again at the age of 26. She finally broke it off and again there was me thinking, 'Oh, woe is me, I will never meet anyone like that again.'

Hearing my lamentations, imagine God (or whoever) appears again and says, 'OK Felix, let me get this straight. You told me Diana was the love of your life and you could only be happy with her, but now you are telling me actually Nicole is the love of your life and you want me to fix it so that you can be with her forever. Right?'

To which I would have replied, 'Yes, yes, just please let me press that button. I was wrong before but am convinced that Nicole is the best partner I will ever have and this is true love. This is the real deal. Where's that button?'

Once again, luckily I wasn't given the chance to press any such button. A couple of years later I met Marie. Marie was a French girl working for an airline company and even prettier and nicer than Nicole. I thought I had found my perfect partner (despite a few glaring problems I was quick to gloss over in my desire to pursue the relationship). Again, about a year down the line, Marie informed me that she was unhappy living in London, was thinking of returning to France, and that anyway we were too different in what we wanted in our lives. We agreed to call it off but it was mostly at her instigation. I was, of course, very upset. Again, I thought, 'OK, OK, I was wrong about Diana, I was even wrong about Nicole, but this time I am *really* convinced that I will never, ever find anyone as good for me as Marie.'

By this time I was beginning to see a pattern. Even though I thought Marie was the best girlfriend for me and the one I thought I would be most happy with, I would have said, if offered, 'You know what, God, no thanks. Every time I *think* I know what's best for me and would have pressed that button, I would have really screwed my life up and missed out on something even better. I admit I do *not know* what is best for me. I just *think* I do. Every time I think, "That's it, I will never find something as good as that", you come and prove me wrong. I think I will just leave it up to you and accept whatever happens.'

A few years later I met Christina, who is now my lovely wife. You guessed it, she is by far the most compatible person for me and I am happier with her than I would have been with anyone else (I dare not big her up any more, in case it looks like I am throwing down the gauntlet to God!).

So stop trying to change the lessons you are being presented with in life. Accept them with humility and gratitude and you just may be surprised, beyond your wildest expectations, where they take you.

In summary

> It's often been observed in times of war and hardship that ordinary people are capable of extraordinary feats of endurance and courage, which they would otherwise never have believed possible.

> We tend to only know our capabilities, resilience and endurance when tested to our near-limits.

> It's best to take the positives from the times when we needed to strive and experience hardship, and ignore the medium by which the striving took place.

> Consider your journey from the possibility of a spiritual perspective. A spiritual perspective refers to a sense of a greater purpose, meaning, consciousness or intelligence working behind the scenes.

> The very fact of acting as if there *should be* meaning and purpose creates meaning and purpose for us.

> We can get so focused on the destination that we forget that the journey is usually more important than the destination.

> Numerous myths from disparate times and regions share fundamental structures and stages and can be collectively looked at as a typical 'hero's journey'.

> The Hero's Journey is a staple archetype and theme in movies that

engages something within us.

> We have a series of developmental tasks to get through in life in order to develop our character. Our challenge is to overcome our early 'passive handicaps' from our childhoods.

> We can make life harder for ourselves by insisting that life should be easy, and taking and protesting when we are compelled to have to strive at things.

> We may feel stuck and victimised in having to repeat certain painful life lessons (the familiar complaint 'Why do these things always happen to me?'), but we get stuck not because of a sadistic or malicious divine puppet-master, but because we refuse to accept the lessons that are presented to us. We tend to want the benefit of the lesson without the cost of the lesson.

> Life is trying to train us to become heroes in our lives and we tend to take offence as to *how* it's trying to turn us into heroes.

> Cultivating hope is a result of being free to experience uncertainty. We do not *know* what is best for us, we just *think* we do.

> Be a hero on your life journey. Be a warrior, not a whiner.

CHAPTER EXERCISE – ADVICE FROM YOUR FUTURE SELF (PART 2)

In the chapter exercise in Chapter 5, I introduced you to the concept of the future self, but only in terms of a short-term perspective, over a few months. Now I'm going to do that for the bigger picture, over several decades.

A 40-year-old advising a 21-year-old

Here are some pointers. If I were advising my 20-something-year-old self, my younger self would say something along the lines of: 'Yes, you are going through one of those hard, testing times. Sorry, no way of getting round that. It couldn't be taught in any other format. Life will have its dramas from time to time, but I'd like you to know this is an important lesson that the future "us" will really appreciate. Thank you for going through it, hang in there, it will all work out.

'Remember you are going through the "testing phase". You are learning to trust in yourself to find a way to resolve this and building resilience in the process.

'Don't worry so much. Life is not about achieving a perfect score-card for efficiency. Enjoy life.

'What's that? You're worried about money? Listen, I've got my best man (me) on it. You're worried about finding a partner? I'm on the case and I've got my best man on that, too.

'All of us in the future are just as dedicated to happiness as you are. If it can be done, it will be done. If it can't be done, then at least you will have tried and known that from experience, and then we will just have to try something else.'

So, one way or another, everything that needs to be addressed will be addressed.

What's left to be anxious about?

My future self would also express some gratitude and appreciation:

'By the way, as a result of all your trials and tribulation, I've sorted out a lot of my baggage. I've got a wonderful partner and career here, and I only got that because of what you are going through in your time. So thanks for all the investments in life you are making right now. They are really paying off, I assure you. In fact they will surpass your expectations.'

Now it's your turn.

Step 1. Consider something in your life that you are currently struggling with. Let's again call this perspective 'position one'.

Step 2. Imagine your future self, perhaps 10 to 15 years ahead, appears in front of you. See this future self as someone who has resolved the struggles you are having in the present and who is at peace with their past. This is 'position two'.

Step 3. Step into this future self in position two, turning to look at your current-day self at position one. What advice would you give to your current-day self about the things he/she feels are so important?

Step 4. Step back into your present-day self in position one and receive that advice and reassurance. How does that change things for you?

PUTTING IT ALL TOGETHER
IN MODERN LIFE

Opportunity is missed by most people because it is dressed in overalls and looks like work.

– Thomas A. Edison

Different types of resilience are required in different developmental stages in our lives – parenting, schooling, relationships, and career. In this chapter, I have also included the areas of sports (for reasons that will be revealed) and New Year's resolutions.

I will be drawing from the previous chapters to offer some general pointers about the type of resilience you will need to develop in each of these areas, based on the most common issues I observe in my cases.

Parenting

It's not easy being a parent. Besides providing physical and financial needs, we also have to train young children to become well-equipped, mentally and emotionally, to face the challenges life will present them. Children need to develop into young adults who can:

- Be distinct individuals aware of their own unique combination of characteristics, creativity and values.
- Be autonomous and self-sufficient – that it to say, can act and think independently, have their own problem-solving skill

sets and be able to navigate their way around the society they live in. They also need to know what they want for themselves.

- Be able to ride through the crises, dramas and vagaries of life without crumbling and being overwhelmed (and be able to handle unexpected success, too, for that matter).

As if that were not hard enough, rallied against these aims are the opposing forces of *intensely protective biological instincts* (which are hell-bent on sparing your child from any pain or problems) and our own emotional baggage, as we try to resolve our own childhood issues through our children.

Some common examples of interfering parental emotional baggage include:

- Spoiling our children by trying to give them everything we wanted when we were their age, but didn't get (trying to resolve unmet needs by proxy).
- Trying to live vicariously through our children (attempting to live experiences via them, which we missed out on in our childhoods, in order to compensate for our loss).
- Giving them all the love we wanted but didn't get – with the result that children may feel smothered.
- Forgetting that they are unique individuals with different preferences, values, needs and aptitudes and instead trying to shape the child in our image. While our wiser self is trying to make our children independent, another part is doing its best to make then dependent on us (because we like to feel involved, needed, important, or we feel we know best).
- We may also tend to see our own qualities reflected in our children, but find it easier to tell them off about these qualities than work on them in ourselves.

In order to achieve our mission as parents we need to adopt all of the seven areas of resilience outlined in this book.

The first step is to become clear about a few things. The first is that (in the vast majority of cases) having children is a choice. You have chosen to turn your life upside-down and change everything with the arrival of one or more children. There will be dramas, there will be heartache, there will be anxiety and uncertainty. There will also be massive benefits.

In Chapter 1, I discussed the concept of:

- Knowing what you want
- Knowing the price for what you want
- Agreeing to pay the price.

This means that when the 'price' for having children appears, we accept it, rather than complain about it. Remember, if you are fortunate enough to have a healthy child through the normal methods, there are other people who would be willing to pay a great deal to be in your shoes. Being a parent really is a privilege.

The second thing is to be clear about your mission in terms of your child's long-term development as an independent, functional individual.

This will help override the in-the-moment, emotional, knee-jerk reaction of trying to spare them from any difficulties, with little regard to what is best for the child's character.

You will of course have to take personal responsibility for your child's development. This is your child and it is not up to his/her teachers to instil manners, duty and values in them. Primarily that is your job.

You will have the instinct to rush in and take over and do everything for your child, but remember that this is disempowering them, and will only teach them to make others responsible for their needs. You ultimately want an empowered child, not a disempowered one.

You also really need to cultivate some state management and stress-coping mechanisms to calm your brain down while you review and consider the bigger picture and most suitable approaches in the pursuit of your child's long-term interests.

I have previously mentioned the concept of being a professional, i.e. adopting a 'professional' parenting hat (see p. 57). I explained that a true professional does not let personal issues interfere with their job. They do their job regardless of how tired they are, whatever else is going on in their life or how they feel about their clients, and they don't take other people's upsets personally. Professionals focus on a higher calling, perhaps on the value they place on doing a job well and professionally. In a parent's case, as mentioned above, it's about the welfare of their child.

School

What advice would I give to a child about coping with school? Phew, the list could be very long. It will have to be focused on a couple of points.

The main one obviously is about cultivating perseverance. Cultivating perseverance, in turn, is more easily done when there is a good reason to endure.

As a student, you will seemingly be asked to sit your bottom down and listen to someone talk about a subject not of your own choosing, which often may not seem relevant to you.

I'm not going to lie to you, that really will often be the case – you will be asked to learn a lot of stuff, a lot of which, in turn, will not end up being directly relevant to you in your life. (Of course, you will also be asked to learn a lot of stuff that could become very relevant in the future. You won't always know!)

Rather than protesting and rejecting all the content you are presented with, I would like you instead to focus on a bigger picture, and consider yourself as a player in a game.

The game is that you do the best you can to study a lot of seemingly unimportant content, because you are being judged on how well you play the game, rather than the content itself. The game is about developing your thinking and problem-solving muscles. If you play the game well, you will have more options and opportunities in your life, which may well allow you to have a far happier future. Usually the better you are at solving problems, the more problems you can solve, and the more rewards you will get.

Imagine a visit from your future self. Your future self tells you that he/she is really in a good position in the future and really enjoying their life. Your future self tells you that he/she is immensely grateful for the perseverance you are displaying at this point, when you cannot see the immediate benefits down the line. That takes a lot of character, and you can rest assured that your investments are paying off in the future.

Your future self may also add that you shouldn't take things so seriously. Nothing is set, and you are still in a process of development. You may not be good academically at first, but you might be later, and the same thing with sports. You might feel like you are short, plump, shy or socially awkward now, but you can develop very differently later on as an adult (I know I did).

Don't take anything as a definitive statement of your capability (e.g. 'I will never be good at maths or languages').

The trick is to take things seriously without taking them *too* seriously. Exam grades, for instance, are important, but we may be putting too much pressure on specific grades (which ironically will undermine our performance).

I remember at age 15 or 16 dreading my big exams (called O-levels in the UK) and putting immense pressure on myself. I truly believed that every grade would determine my life. Now I struggle to remember what subjects I did, let alone the grades.

Strive to do the best you can, but remember it is not a matter of life or death. You can find success in many ways, but since you have to do exams, you might as well do them as well as you can and to the best of your ability (without stressing).

A few years ago, an email about 'Rules For Kids' found its way into my inbox. I believe the original source was Charles J. Sykes, who wrote

50 Rules Kids Won't Learn in School, and I've summarised the gist of his message below. While it sounds a bit harsh, a couple of interesting points are mentioned (as a parent, I particularly like point 7!).

RULE 1: Life is not fair and you'd better get used to it (a point we all agree on).

RULE 2: The world doesn't care about your self-esteem. The world will expect you to accomplish something before it will congratulate you.

RULE 3: You won't make a lot of money straight out of high school. You will have to earn your success.

RULE 4: If you think your teacher is tough, wait till you get a boss.

RULE 5: Flipping burgers or ringing up groceries is not beneath your dignity. Your grandparents had a different word for burger flipping; they called it opportunity.

RULE 6: Don't whine about your mistakes – learn from them.

RULE 7: Before you were born, your parents weren't boring parents. They got that way from paying your bills, cleaning your clothes and listening to you talk about yourself. Think about that before you judge them.

RULE 8: Your school may have done away with winners and losers, but life has not.

RULE 9: Life is not divided into semesters. You don't get summers off and very few employers are interested in helping you find yourself. You'll have to do that on your own time.

RULE 10: Television is NOT real life. In real life people actually have to leave the coffee shop and go to jobs.

RULE 11: Be nice to nerds. Chances are you'll end up working for one.

Sports

I've included the topic of sports here for a number of reasons. The first is that, in terms of school sports, you might have to put up with doing a sports subject that is not of your choosing, in a similar way to having to tolerate doing academic subjects not of your choosing.

Nowadays being forced to participate in a sport you dislike is less of an issue than it used to be at school, but the same principles apply. Just as seemingly irrelevant academic subjects stimulate your problem-solving muscles, engaging in sport helps you to increase your endurance and perseverance muscles. Moreover, studies show that good physical health tends to also improve cognitive or mental health.

One of the main points in this book is that adversity in the right balance is good for you. It makes you grow. The trick is to artificially induce adversity in a balanced way, so we can be ready for it when it really hits, in the same way that an inoculation (basically dead germs) trains your immune system to fight the real disease when it comes, or the way armed forces train do war games as part of their training.

We get to be wise by being tested by something that stimulates wisdom. In that spirit – of seeing challenges as growth opportunities – you can, if you wish, take advantage of the excellent medium of sports to face and overcome many of your innate fears.

When I was 12, I went to boarding school. I heard that in the next term we would have to do at least one two-kilometre run per week. I was dreading that. I had never run any real distance in my life and quite rightly feared for my stamina. I remember that during the first runs we did, I had to frequently stop, huffing and puffing. By the end of the term I was able to complete the course without stopping and lost the weight around my stomach.

The next year I wanted to win a special 'house tie' (really for the status rather than the tie – these things are important to a young boy). A house tie could be won for distinguished achievement in sports. Since

I still couldn't understand how to play rugby or cricket, and wasn't in those sports teams, I had to turn to running. I would get a house tie if I did the most runs in a term. One week I ran the course nine separate times. I was even showing new boys how to run it and pace themselves. By the end of the spring term, I had run the course nearly 40 times, won my award and was as fit as a fiddle.

Running no longer held any fear for me, because I became desensitised to the pain of running that distance.

The next year I was allowed to start karate, which helped me work on desensitising myself to a new range of fears – my beliefs about experiencing physical pain and threat of harm. Many times during my training, I had to face up to an opponent who was bigger and stronger than me. After our sparring was over I usually came off thinking, 'Well, that wasn't as bad as I feared. I thought I would get killed, but I managed to hold my own.' Occasionally I even had the satisfaction of seeing the person I felt trepidation about fighting having the same look on their face when they met me.

In addition, before we got to the actual training in karate, we would do a 20-minute warm-up, with press-ups, push-ups and stretching. It can be a bit boring and tedious, but your body soon adapts and learns next time, as you enter the training area that, yeah, it's going to be a bit boring and 'painful' for a while, but then it's over and you get to learn the cool stuff. This sort of thing helps a person to voluntarily take on some pain in the present, in order to feel the benefits in the future.

Nowadays I no longer do contact sports, I just work out at my local gym.

Let's face it – going to the gym can be tedious, dull and hard work. But what helps get me though it are these precedents from my past: 'Yeah, it's a bit boring and dull for a while, but then it's over and you get to the benefits.'

I'm also pretty certain that these early lessons helped me get through my initial six-year training in psychology. Six years is a long time to be an impoverished student in your late twenties. You really have to focus on getting through the dull stuff (exams) in order to get the career at the end of the tunnel.

If contact sports are not your cup of tea, there are many others that will test you to overcome pain in its many different forms. My other favourite sport recommendation is dancing. Dancing can be so much fun that you don't even realise you have just done a serious aerobic workout, and again there are a whole range of spin-off benefits, including better sleep, more confidence and an endorphin high.

I'm pretty sure our bodies crave a lot more physical activity than most of them currently get. If you have eliminated all sports from your life, I would strongly recommend that you research and find some sort of physical activity to engage in. This will help you develop resilience in another important way.

Relationships

Of course, whole books could be written about resilience in relationships.

In terms of the lessons covered in this book, the most important areas in the context of developing resilience in relationships are:

> Attitude (Chapter 1)

> Taking personal responsibility (Chapter 2)

> Being aware of taking things personally (Chapters 2 and 6)

> Being aware of the role of stress (Chapter 6, and throughout)

Entering into a relationship is a big commitment in our lives – not quite the same upheaval as having a child, but still quite a change. Suddenly it's not just about us any more, doing what we want, when we want. We have another person to consider and consult with in the decision-making process. There are another set of needs to take into account.

Once the honeymoon period has worn off, we realise that maintaining a relationship takes effort and application. It needs continual watering, just like a plant.

Again, if we want all the good stuff from a relationship (the companionship, laughs, physical intimacy, sharing of chores, someone to support us if things get tough), we've got to pay the price. And doing this is a choice.

There will be constraints on our freedom and autonomy. You will have to keep someone in the loop about your plans so that they can plan accordingly too. You may feel like switching off and going on stand-by when your partner wants to talk and bond. Your partner may be going through a personal drama, when you feel tired and are thinking, 'I really don't need this right now.'

There will be differences in values.

There will be difference in understanding and processing, even of the same information.

You will both act out your emotional baggage on each other.

In short, it will be tough sometimes. There will be highs and lows.

I think a good start, therefore, would be to know the price for a relationship, accept it, and be willing to nurture the relationship so that it remains healthy.

Taking personal responsibility means being an active participant in the relationship. Unlike your first relationship, with your parents, where you were passive and someone else was responsible for meeting all your needs, as an adult you have a responsibility to meet your own needs in your relationship as well as that of your partner (your partner, of course, has the same responsibility).

By looking after your own needs, I mean don't suffering in silence if something is not working for you. Your partner can't read your mind and they need to know your status.

You will have to keep your partner happy, too, if you want them to stick around. I see a lot of people who complain about their partner, but do very little to improve the situation. It's as if they feel that 'it's ALL his/her fault'. They are waiting for their partner to fix everything while they sit passively on the sidelines. Obviously that is not going to help. Taking personal responsibility means:

> Owning the problem (make it your duty to identify and clarify the unmet need).
> Deciding what needs to be done instead (that involves both of you!).
> Communicating the needs to your partner (in neutral, non-accusatory language).

If you both choose to take personal responsibility for your relationship being a happy one, then you have a fighting change of creating that. If only one of you chooses to do all the work, your chances are halved.

Obviously if both of you leave it up to the other to solve the problems, the chances are zero.

A lot of relationships fail due to poor communication. This is the life-blood of most relationships and simply involves sufficiently sharing your internal status with your partner – expressing your likes, dislikes, opinions and feelings about your interactions with your partner and things around you. In this way your partner gets to know you, the real you, and also can track things are.

Communication also refers to practical things like planning and arrangements. If you stop communicating, you are creating a vacuum of information, one your partner is likely to fill with their worst fears.

Taking things personally is an extension of taking personal responsibility. Often our partner will not say things in an offensive way, but we will interpret things that way and blame them. We have to take responsibility for our interpretation. In particular, we tend to take things personally when we are stressed. Stress really is our common enemy, yet we will attribute the hostility and problems caused by stress to our relationship or our partner's personality traits (e.g. he/she is always arguing when the problem might be that 'we are both really stressed').

So be clearer about when you have an underlying unresolved stress problem, as opposed to a relationship problem.

Career

Different kinds of resilience will be needed to clarify and pursue your career and then, of course, to handle the pressures of working in that career. Of particular importance are cultivating resilience in persevering through uncertain times, and trusting in yourself.

Recently I saw a young man in his mid-twenties for depression, whom I will call Peter. Peter came to see me because of intense procrastination and avoidance issues, leading to an overall feeling of depression. He was unemployed and desperately wanted a creative job in the online gaming industry, but would really struggle with completing applications because of his fear of failure.

Consequently he only managed to complete and submit a few job applications in time, which meant that he was putting all his eggs in one basket. Because he ended up attaching so much importance to one or two applications over a long period of time, he ended up creating pressure and performance anxiety for himself – which he then sought to avoid.

The first thing I noticed about Peter was that he was using pain as his internal motivator. The pain of doing his applications dominated until the even greater pain of *not* doing his application and *not* knowing if he would have missed out on a great job occasionally took over and dominated instead. Either way, pain is pain, and it was present throughout his system, taking its toll.

The first thing I had to do was deflate the importance he had attached to each application. Peter was in the habit of thinking, 'Everything is riding on this, I only want this job and no other, and if I don't get it I'll die penniless, alone and hated by everyone.'

Peter wanted everything in one go or he would get disheartened. It

168

was as if, for him, there were just two steps involved: 'Here I am looking at the job I want' and 'Over there is the job I want and I don't have it'. Looking at things this way makes it a case of pass/fail and overlooks any sense of a process at work. The truth is that usually there will be a series of stepping-stones before we reach our destination. While there may be many individual stones that make the whole thing look daunting and hard, each stone is actually quite achievable.

Consider for a moment the process involved in making the humble cup of tea.

If you had to explain the entire process for making a cup of tea to an alien who has never observed this process before, and had to quickly guess at how many steps were involved, how many would you guess? Probably five or six?

Actually there are more like 30. For instance:

1. Take kettle
2. Take kettle to tap. Turn tap, fill kettle.
3. Take out the teabag container and place on table.
4. Take out the sugar container and place on table.
5. Open fridge.
6. Take out milk … etc.

Every time you make a cup of tea you are achieving more than thirty little tasks. Do you ever baulk at all the steps, thinking, 'I want a cup of tea, but I've got to do 30 things, that's just too much!'

Hardly. You take each easy step one at a time until you reach your destination.

Neither do you think that making a cup of tea simply involves just two steps: 'Here I am looking at the cup of tea I want' and 'Over there is the tea'. You intuitively know that there are more than two steps involved in the process.

If it takes more than 30 steps to make a cup of tea, then surely finding a job can take many dozens of little individual, achievable steps until there is a fruitful hit.

Using the analogy of the stepping-stone, I coached Peter to be more creative in his job-hunting, doing peripheral jobs and tasks in the gaming industry while working his way towards his ideal position. Once he saw it more as a process, he allowed himself to relax into it and just focus on one thing at a time, working on achieving his next step.

I also had to work on Peter's self-beliefs. Peter believed he possessed good qualities for the industry, but worried whether he would be able to convey these qualities and do them justice. He needed to believe in his ability to do them justice. I used the tools described in Chapter 5 to coach him into building up his confidence.

Ultimately confidence comes from *doing*. Nothing convinces like reality, i.e. doing something and achieving results. We just need to get people past the fear and avoidance stage into the doing and achieving stage so they can experience that for themselves.

The wonderful thing about attention, focus and application is that it can be thought of a little bit like a magic wand. Whatever problem you point your magic wand of attention and application at begins to shrink, dissolve and disappear. Funny that.

Instead we can get into the habit of spending more energy avoiding pointing our magic wand at the problem than would ever be needed to solve the problem itself. If a given problem takes 10 units of energy to solve by focus and application, we think nothing of spending thousands of units trying to avoid the pain of doing 10.

The fog metaphor

If you find yourself in an uncertain position, such as job hunting in tough economic times, you may be cheered up by the following analogy.

Imagine you have been invited to a party five miles away. You get into your car to drive there but there is a dense fog so you can only see the next 20 feet in front. Would you say to yourself, 'It's no good, I can't see the final destination, I'm going to go back home?'

No. You would drive on, knowing that as you get through the next 20 feet, the next 20 feet after that will make itself known to you, then the next 20 feet after that, and the next 20. You simply trust (without any guarantee) that you don't need to know the answers up front to arrive where you want. All you have to do is see and deal with the next phase of the journey as you get to it.

For that matter, if you were to find yourself taking a wrong turn into a cul-de-sac or dead end, you wouldn't think to yourself, 'Well, I've made a mistake so that's it, I guess I should stay here and beat myself up, or speculate how I can now define my life as that guy who tried but failed.' You would simply reverse, backtrack, gather your bearings and proceed onward to your destination.

New Year's resolutions

A bit of a lightweight topic to end on, I know, but I've included this because modest resolutions – whether made in the new year or not – offer a testing ground for you to apply some of the principles in this book and experience a change in your typical determination and perseverance.

I was recently asked by a journalist why people typically give up their new year's resolutions within three weeks. He asked me whether perhaps it was because the targets people set themselves were too unrealistic

I replied that the targets set may be realistic, but that it's a lack of commitment to follow through and planning that makes people stumble and give up. Most people want to give up smoking, lose weight or go to the gym, set a resolution to do so, and that's it. They have done nothing else other than *hope* they will have enough will power to pull through or that, on that date, they will magically feel different about their old habits and change.

These kind of decisions tend to be doomed to failure. The best decisions require elements that by now you will be very familiar with:

> Clarification. Knowing what you want and why you want it. This also leads to a change in values and the meaning of the desired behaviour.

> Attitude. Taking personal responsibility for your results.

It is clear that you cannot keep doing the same thing you have in the past and expect a different outcome. If you want to change, then at some point it's crunch time and you have to pay your dues. Choose to pay these dues and be prepared to do what is needed to get the outcome you desire. Otherwise you will just make yet another commitment to put it off and have the same failure again next year.

The time for change is now. Don't put off the hard work for some future you, who will pass it off to yet another, more distant future you. That is not commitment to results. That is just hoping some future self will finally have the willpower to do the right thing. But guess what? With that kind of attitude, your future self will feel exactly the same as you do now.

If you want to change, you have to accept responsibility. Take this commitment seriously; don't just treat it as another vain hope. By taking results seriously, you will actually start to plan for success, e.g. making the time to go to the gym (as opposed to hoping you will get round to finding some time), and will plan for getting over setbacks, too.

Now when you consider any new resolutions, you will be armed with knowledge and tools to help you stick to your decisions. And remember that success also generates further success. The more success you have in one area, the more confidence you will have to apply your formulas for success in other areas, too.

EPILOGUE

So we have come to the end, dear reader. We've gone through a series of steps that, if you choose to take them on board and apply them, will make you wiser and more resilient, and enable you to get more out of your life.

You have learnt about adopting the right attitude to foster resilience, about how to persevere and become more irreverent in the face of obstacles, and how to understand and manage your emotional state. As you do these things, you will find that your trust in yourself increases.

Overall I hope you also have gained a sense of accepting the life track you find yourself on – a life track that perhaps you did not want to happen, but one that needed to happen so you could learn a lesson you can't even comprehend right now!

This is your character-building time. This is the time to persevere in something, when you have no way of seeing into the future and realising the benefits. You just have to trust that the process works that way for many, many people and so will work for you.

I wish you every success in your personal hero's journey, and remember – you don't have to do it alone. Others have been on this path before you, and left signs and hints for those that will follow after them. If you get stuck, check out what others who have been in your position have to say on the matter. If you want to make it easier, learn from the experience of others who have been there before you.

Then, in time, you can be the teacher for others, too.

Contacting the author

If you want to share your personal stories of resilience or have any comments about this book, please contact me at felix@treatmentsforthemind.co.uk, or visit my website: www.treatmentsforthemind.co.uk.

QUESTIONNAIRE:

HOW RESILIENT ARE YOU?

The following questions will assess how you are currently dealing with stress in different areas of your life. For your own benefit, answer truthfully – in terms of how you *actually* respond, not how you should respond or how you would like to respond. Honest answers allow you to properly gauge where you need to focus your change work. Comments will follow at the end of the questionnaire.

1. Attitude

i) When it's time to meet your needs in the context of having a good career, relationship, project, recreation time, etc, you:

    a)   Go with the flow and see what happens.

    b)   Take time to think about what it is you want.

    c)   Rely on someone else you trust to tell you what to do.

    d)   Complain that your life is not the way it should be.

    e)   See what your friends are doing and do what they do.

ii) If you are on the path you want, but it involves hard work, you:

    a)   Feel despondent and down about your situation.

    b)   Complain about the stress this path subjects you to.

    c)   Start to doubt your decision.

    d)   Accept it is difficult and get on with it.

    e)   Look for sympathy and comfort from others.

iii) Your choice of path is influenced mostly by:

    a)   Money.

    b)   Status.

    c)   Convenience.

    d)   Creativity.

    e)   Security.

2. Personal responsibility

i) When someone complains about their situation, you:

    a)   Find it interesting but remain uninvolved.

    b)   Feel a strong compulsion to take over and make it better for them.

    c)   Remain uninterested and uninvolved.

    d)   Empathise, offer advice but accept that they have to find their own way.

    e)   Want to comfort and console them.

ii) In any altercation with another person, you:

    a)   Empathise with the other person's valid points, but also respect your own valid points.

    b)   Feel the need to win (or not lose) the argument, regardless of the points are being made.

    c)   Blame the other person for being so unreasonable.

    d)   Always agree with their criticisms of you.

    e)   Calm down and see their point of view later on.

iii) When you realise you are not where you want to be in life, you:

    a)   Feel sad or hurt.

    b)   Feel God is punishing you.

    c)   Feel you are just unlucky.

    d)   Feel others deserve more than you.

e) Assess the difference between where you are and where you want to be, and seek to close the gap.

3. Perseverance

i) When the going gets tough in a desired endeavour, you:
a) Complain about the problems unfairly dumped on you.
b) Think of how you can get out of the situation.
c) Put off the work until the next day.
d) Get discouraged quite easily.
e) Question your decision to be on this path.
f) Stick with it until the goal is achieved.

ii) When doing work, you:
a) Do a good dose of work, then take short breaks.
b) Power through, working until you are exhausted.
c) Suddenly find other non-urgent tasks to do.
d) Check your emails or Facebook every five minutes.
e) Plan a time to work and a time to play.

4. Being Irreverent in the Face of Obstacles

i) When coming up against an obstacle, you:
a) Assume you will be unable to resolve it.
b) Immediately look for help from others.
c) Make light of it.
d) Keep an open mind as you approach it and see what happens.
e) Listen to others telling you that you're not good at dealing with those kinds of obstacles.

ii) When an obstacle is in the form of an ongoing process (e.g. going to the gym, doing a project, admin), you:
a) Take action to get it out of the way as soon as possible.

b)   Coach yourself through it ('look, it will be tough, but then it will get easier').

c)   Have to mentally steel yourself every time to face it.

d)   Put it off until the last minute, relying on fear of consequences to motivate you.

5. Trusting in Self

i) When considering how much you trust yourself, you:

a)   Fundamentally assume that negative outcomes will happen (i.e. assuming there will be more problems and heartache down the line, you are already worrying about how you will cope).

b)   Fundamentally assume positive outcomes will happen (beliving it will work out in the end).

c)   A little bit of each, depending on the situation.

d)   Assume it will be OK as long as someone else will be there with you.

e)   Blame yourself for not being stronger or more capable.

6. State Management

i) When you have a difference of opinion with someone, you reply with:

a)   'Why are you being this way?'

b)   'What's wrong with you?'

c)   'Why are you having a go at me?'

d)   Or do you put aside the style of communication to get to the point?

ii) When you feel angry or frustrated, you:

a)   Primarily seek to express your anger or frustration, then pick up the pieces for any damage caused.

b)   Shy away from all conflict.

c)   Feel determined to seek satisfaction and vengeance on whoever 'made' you angry.

d)   Assess the situation to see if it's 'worth it' (getting involved).

e)   Take a deep breath and coach yourself to consider the most effective response.

Results

Rather than basing results along the lines of 'score between 1–3 and you are a resilient person, score between 4–6 and you are an un-resilient person', my comments are broader and a bit more philosophical. I'm not a great fan of labels and pigeon-holing people. You might be very resilient in some areas, but not yet in others. The aim is to give you pointers about where to focus your attention.

Section 1: Attitude

Of the options presented in question (i), option b (*take time to think about what it is you want*) would be the most mature response, with d (*complain that your life is not the way it should be*) being the most immature response. I would recommend that you consider your values and needs, and then make a plan to meet them.

Copying someone else who has taken the time to think about their values because it spares you the hard work of thinking for yourself is never advisable. You are not a clone of any other person. They will have different values and preferences than you. Maturity calls for making yourself the 'measure of yourself' rather than copying someone else (for a guide to clarifying your values, see Chapter 3 of my first book, *Take Charge of Your Life With NLP*, published by Vermilion, 2011).

If you chose option a (*go with the flow and see what happens*), while a 'go with the flow' mentality is sometimes appropriate, it can lead to a kind of passivity where you always go with the general consensus rather than focusing on your values. If you chose c (*rely on someone else you trust to tell you what to do*), then you still have not learnt to trust your own judgement or are unaware of your emotional needs. Again this suggests a need for more maturity in this area, as relying on others to tell you what you need is behaviour more appropriate for a child than an adult. You will need to learn how to focus on discerning your own needs.

Regarding question (ii), the most useful response would be option d (*accept it is difficult and get on with it*). If you chose option a (*feel despondent and down about your situation*) then you are too easily discouraged or overwhelmed by challenges, which suggests a lack of trust and self-belief. If you chose option b (*complain about the stress this path subjects you to*) then you are operating in victim mode rather than creator mode. Start adopting the creator position more. If you chose c (*start to doubt your decision*), then that again indicates a lack of self-belief or knowing what you really want. If you know what you want, then desire for your goal generates commitment and dedication. If you chose e (*look for sympathy and comfort from others*), this may indicate a victim mentality, where you seek comfort for the hardships (which is a way of avoiding paying the necessary price needed), or again a lack of self-belief in your ability to handle the challenges facing you.

Regarding question (iii), the aim of this question is more to nudge you into clarifying your highest values about your career path, and then to asses whether those values are being fulfilled. My preference is for a path that expresses creativity. In my experience, people who are able to match their internal creativity with an external outlet are the most satisfied and fulfilled, even when money or income is not very high in such paths. It does depend on the individual, though. There is no one right answer. Convenience or security might well be the most important consideration for you. My least preferred option is 'status', because that is about indulging the ego at the expense of healthier needs.

Section 2: Personal Responsibility

Question (i) gives an indication of how responsible you feel for others. If you answered a (*find it interesting but remain uninvolved*) then that may suggest you have good awareness or respect for what is your problem to solve, and what is another's, although a little more empathy might be advisable. Obviously if someone is genuinely struggling and needs help, it's good to offer assistance. If you *feel a strong compulsion to take over and make it better for them* (answer b), then watch yourself. You may be a bit of a compulsive interventionist or rescuer. You mean well, but you might be cheating someone out of important developmental lessons, or training them to become dependent on you (while you feel good about your rescuing). If you chose *remain uninterested and uninvolved*, then you are firmly of the belief that 'it's not my problem, nothing to do with me', which, while technically correct, suggests you probably need to work on your empathy.

Option d is my preferred response. It's possible to have compassion, empathy and understanding, without being either a heroic rescuer or a person who washes their hands of any matter that does not directly concern them.

If you chose answer e (*want to comfort and console them*) then be aware of a possible martyr tendency, or a desire to always make things right. Rather than saying, 'Hush, it's OK, you don't have to do anything you don't want to', it might be more useful to give them a pep talk and let them have another try at their endeavour. Recently I treated a very pretty 12-year-old girl for difficulty with eating foods. She ate an amazingly unhealthy and limited diet, but her mother and grandmother were completely under her spell. At the first sign of discomfort, they would rush to the girl's aid and remind her that she did not have to face any difficult choices. Consequently I expect the young girl will grow up expecting that that is an appropriate formula for dealing with life's problems.

Regarding question (ii), my preferred answer would be option a (*empathise with the other person's valid points but also respect your own valid points*). If you chose (ii), *feel the need to win or not lose the arguments regardless of the points being made,* then ego, pride or defensiveness is taking over and not doing you any favours in the long run. You might technically win every argument, but at the cost of alienating your friends, family or partner. Would you rather be right or happy?

Answer c (*blame the other person for being so unreasonable*) is something we can all do in the heat of the moment, as long as afterwards we take stock of things and put things right. Of course it is possible that you are dealing with a genuinely unreasonable person, but this question is more of a prompt to bring your awareness to the possibility that you are making others overly responsible for all communication problems. Answer e (*always agree with others' criticisms of you*) suggests you are overly responsible for the reactions or feelings of others. You never take your own side, because you defer to the opinions of others, whom you trust and esteem more. You will need to do some self-esteem building. Answer f (*calm down and see their point of view later on*) is my second preferred approach and a good step in the right direction – calming down the amygdala and then engaging the frontal lobes (thinking brain) to make a more accurate assessment of the situation.

Regarding question (iii), you will have undoubtedly guessed by now that I will recommend option e (*assess the difference between where you are and where you want to be and seek to close the gap*), unless you haven't been paying attention at all in this book! Choosing any of answers a, b, c or d suggests a tendency toward a prevailing victim mindset that will not help you to make things better. You can either take things personally and indulge in self-pity and self-comforting behaviours, or take the creator position and do something about it.

Section 3: Perseverance

Regarding question (i), I assume you will have guessed again that my main recommendation will be option f (*persevering with a goal until it is achieved*). Choosing option a (*complain about the problems unfairly dumped on you*) suggests you adopt the victim mentality instead of a steadfast, persevering attitude. Option b (*think of how you can get out of the situation*) suggest an avoidant reflexive response, either due to looking for the quick fix or easy path, or because you doubt your abilities to persevere. Option c (*put off the work for the next day*) is a step up from the previous option, in that you do have the best intentions to do the necessary work, but you never quite get around to it. This indicates an underlying problem with procrastination. Option d (*get discouraged quite easily*) is avoidance due to a lack of sufficient self-belief. Option e (*you question your decision to be on this path*) means you doubt yourself, also due to insufficient self-belief.

The only way to grow confidence in yourself is to allow yourself to face your challenges and find ways to overcome them. Avoidance keeps you stuck in inadequate self-belief.

Regarding question (ii), my ideal answer would be option e, followed by a. Occasionally there is a need, due to the sheer workload on that day, to power through until you can take no more. The main point of this question is to draw your attention to the presence of distractions (answers c and d). If you plan for sufficient work and recharge time, you will find there will be less of a reliance on distractions to justify taking some breaks.

Section 4: Being Irreverent in the Face of Obstacles

Regarding question (i), my preferred response would be option d (*keep an open mind as you approach an obstacle and see what happens*). Many times in the past I have overestimated an obstacle, and then when I have got around to facing it and overcoming it, I berated myself for not facing it sooner, because it was far easier than I thought it would be.

Sometimes I also like to make light of an impending obstacle (option c), as this provides a morale booster, while being careful to respect it and not dismiss the work needed. Either answer would be a step in the right direction.

The remaining answers would again demonstrate fear and avoidance based on the usual suspects – lack of self-belief, 'pain' aversion and looking to others to rescue us.

Regarding question (ii), my preferred responses are a (*take action as soon as you can to try and get it out of the way*) followed by b (*coach yourself through it*). Having to mentally steel yourself every time you face a persistent challenge (option c) means that at least you are facing the challenge, but it does suggest a failure to learn or adapt somewhere along the chain, so that momentum keeps having to be regenerated instead of being able to go on auto-pilot.

Putting things off until the last minute, relying on fear of consequences to motivate you (option d), is obviously the most painful and least efficient response, requiring the most attention to change.

Section 5: Trusting in Self

Regarding question (i), option a suggests you are fundamentally pessimistic about your chances of success, and need some confidence-building exercises.

If you chose option b or c, then I am pleased. They are my preferred options, especially b.

If you chose *assume it will be OK as long as someone else will be there with you* (option d), then you still have to learn that you do not need someone else to hold your hand forever. Trust yourself to manage and cope on your own or you will be unwittingly disempowering yourself.

Blaming yourself for not being stronger or more capable (option e) is a waste of time and indicative of 'bad worry' as opposed to 'good worry'. You either have all the understanding, capabilities or internal resources you need to solve a problem, or you don't. If you don't, then focus on acquiring them, not blaming yourself for not having them in the first place.

Section 6: State Management

Regarding question (i), either of the first three options (*'Why are you being this way?'* or *'What's wrong with you?'* or *'Why are you having a go at me?'*) indicate that you take things too personally and/or get overly defensive. In doing so, you are likely to overlook the point being made by the other person and instead end up arguing about how you are arguing. I would suggest that you focus on addressing, acknowledging and validating the point made by the other person first, and then making constructive feedback on how they could have communicated the point better in hindsight.

Regarding question (ii), my preferred responses would be e (*take a deep breath and coach yourself to consider the most effective response*) followed by c (*assess the situation to see if it's 'worth it'*), either of which suggests an intent to maintain a cool head and appraise the situation in a level-headed way.

If you answered option a (*primarily seek to express your anger or frustration, then pick up the pieces for any damage caused*), you may have a little bit of a temper or anger management problem to work on. With training, you can condition yourself to interrupt your old anger indulgence.

If you answered option b (*shy away from all conflict*), that suggests a failure to learn or adapt in your approach to handling conflict. Sometimes you do have to fight for your rights or the rights of others. Avoiding conflict because it makes you feel uncomfortable is not taking responsibility for protecting your rights. Work on removing the blocks in place, then experiment with a way of addressing conflict that inspires you with the confidence to use it.

If you answered c, then stop giving yourself over to the dark side and indulging your vengeance fantasies to get even with everyone. Remember, not everything that happens to you is about you. Practise exercises in this book about seeing the bigger picture and rising above the ego's desire to smash anyone who offends us into the ground.

A SIX-STEP PLAN:
FOR BUILDING RESILIENCE

This is a very, very simple plan. For six days of the week, I recommend you focus on one of the six main principles outlined in this book. Go through the summaries at the end of each chapter and find some points you would like to cultivate. Pick one or two, then devote yourself to applying those points at every available opportunity throughout the day. The next day, do the same thing for the next principle. Sunday is a day of rest and reflection.

At the end of the six days, you can start all over again for the following week, using either the same aspects (if you want more practise and reinforcement in these areas) or, if you feel you have sufficiently mastered them, moving on to the next set of points you would like to focus on

Day	Principle to focus on:
MON	Attitude
TUESDAY	Personal responsibility
WEDNESDAY	Perseverance
THURSDAY	Being irreverent in the face of obstacles
FRIDAY	Trusting in self
SATURDAY	State management

UK £12.99